MARIJUANA GROWING SECRETS

THE ULTIMATE BEGINNER'S GUIDE TO PERSONAL AND MEDICAL MARIJUANA CULTIVATION INDOORS AND OUTDOORS. DISCOVER HOW TO GROW TOP QUALITY WEED AND ADVANCED CANNABIS GROWING TIPS

CALVIN NEWMAN

CONTENTS

INTRODUCTION

Just like any other kind of gardening, cannabis growing is a skill that is developed over time. Think of cultivating Marijuana as a rewarding hobby that doubles up as a great business opportunity. It is not only easy to learn but also takes a lifetime to master.

Well, don't get me wrong; I am not saying that you should not get started. There is no reason for you to get intimidated. One thing I love about the cultivation of Marijuana is that the process is straightforward and inexpensive.

One of the best places to start your Marijuana growing journey is to understand the fundamentals of Marijuana cultivation. When you make informed decisions every step of the way, you will have the upper hand at maximizing yields. This is precisely what this guide will help you achieve – an excellent knowledge based on becoming an expert marijuana gardener.

The very first thing you need to think about is where you would like to set up your growing area/space. Well, just because you are thinking "indoors" does not mean that you must have a typical grow room. If you don't have so much space to spare in your home, you don't have to worry because you can still do your grow outdoors – where you have ease of access while still maintaining discretion from nosey neighbors.

If you choose to do indoor growing of Marijuana and you don't have so much space inside your home, you can do it even in an old cabinet in the garage, tent, cabinet, or an unfinished basement. The most important thing is that space is enough to accommodate all your growing equipment required.

If you are just getting started, it is essential to start small. Starting small makes the setting up less costly. Additionally, you make it easier for yourself to monitor a few plants as a beginner. In case you make a mistake, it is also less expensive. As a beginner, there are several challenges you might encounter during your cultivation – like pests and diseases – which ultimately might result in the loss of your marijuana plants. If you have a small space, you will lose to say five plants, which is less expensive compared to losing 50 plants.

That said, it is essential to think big when allocating space for your cultivation. As yourself whether you have enough room for the lights, fans, ducting, and equipment. Do you have some elbow room to move around once the plants are grown? Bear in mind that once the cannabis plants grow, they triple in size and need space.

You may be wondering, "what are some of the fundamentals of growing marijuana?"

Well, here is what you need to know;

Light: If you are growing your plants outdoors, then this should not be a big problem as you depend on night and day for natural regulation of light required by your plants. If you are going to cultivate healthy marijuana plants indoors, you must consider over 12-hours of light in every 24-hr period. Growing indoors means that you have to control light.

Growing medium: when doing organic growing, you will need some soil each time. However, one thing you must bear in mind is that soil is not the only choice. There are neutral mediums that are entirely nutrient-dependent or purely hydroponic – do not use mediums at all.

Air: for your marijuana plants to be healthy, they require a proper gaseous exchange. Unlike outdoors, where this is not an issue of concern, indoor cannabis plants need to take in the fresh air every time. A lack of proper gas exchange channels will encourage molds, pests' weak growths, or even stunted plant growths.

Water: just like every living thing, cannabis plants require water for growth. For outdoor plants, you can depend on rainfall or irrigation. Indoors, water is an essential medium for carrying nutrients. Note that unmodified water plays a vital role in flushing hydroponic and soilless systems. You must ensure the pH of the water is right. Hence, you must have a good pH meter as part of your comprehensive grow kit.

Temperature: while Marijuana is a very hardy plant that survives cold and heat, the truth is that it too can get stressed and not thrive in extremes. Trust me; it can freeze or boil to death! The good thing with growing them indoors is that you can set the required temperatures using fans, heating, and cooling mats, as well as air conditioning units. Realize that lights generate heat too, and that needs to be vented well.

Nutrients: this is the fuel cannabis plants require to fuel growth. Your growth medium rich with compost, living organisms, minerals, and vitamins supply your cannabis plants with adequate foods for their entire lifecycle. The plant's lifeblood is a pre-formulated nutrient blend customized for cannabis if you choose to work with hydroponic systems.

That said, this guide will help you ensure that all the fundamentals are taken care of throughout the lifecycle of your cannabis plant – from vegetative, flowering, and fruiting stages. By the time you are done reading this book, you will not only know about growing but also harvesting and keeping proper amounts on hand throughout the year.

Trust me; this is your key to unlocking big-time yields.

Read on to find out more!

1

CHOOSE THE STRAIN

When preparing to plant your marijuana strains, whether indoors or outdoors, you must clear a space for the growth area. Whether it is choosing the kind of grow lights to go for or the coveted strains for your setup, you must understand that prepping each grows is critical for your gardening success.

Throughout this chapter, we will discuss how you can choose your strains before getting started with planting. Realize that different plants are different, which requires that you prepare the right growing environment for each strain.

For instance, cannabis Sativa plants are known to grow tall and give off smaller buds during harvest times. Cookie strains and Kushes, on the other hand, tend to grow bushy and give fatter buds during harvest times. The difference in their growth indicates that each one of them requires a unique growing environment, training methods, and nutrition for them to give the kind of yield you desire.

This is why we recommend that you perform thorough research on the kind of strain you wish to plant so that you can go for the best strain you can give the appropriate growth conditions. Luckily for you, you will not have to go to a library to get this information because this book offers you comprehensive coverage of what you need to know – all-under one roof!

Are you not sure what to look for?

Here are some of the key aspects you must consider when looking for the perfect strain for you to grow;

THE OVERALL SIZE OF THE FULL-GROWN PLANT

Just as we have mentioned above, the size of your strain should be your guide when choosing the grow room/space size and the lighting required.

Room size

Knowing the full-grown size of the marijuana strain you want to plant goes a long way in determining the kind of space you need to use. The size of the plant also gives you an idea of how many plants you can grow in a given size, and hence the expected yield.

Lighting

Once you know the size of the plant you want to grow, the next thing is to figure out the amount of lighting it requires. If your plants get too strong light, they might fry to death. On the other hand, if the light is weak, your plants risk not growing at all. Based on the plant size and how many your grow space can take, you can easily determine the amount of light needed and how to position your plants in your grow area.

Average yields

You must have an idea of the yield your strain of choice gives as far as size, quality, and quantity goes. Take a minute to ask yourself these questions;

Will the harvest consist of smaller or fatter buds? If the expected buds are bigger, then this means that they require more nutrition and lighting. You must know what to get in terms of the harvest to ensure that you offer all your plants the time and nutrition they need.

How much yield should you expect? Based on research, the expected yield is based on how well you care for your plants. However, there is a realistic expectation you must keep in mind during growing. In other words, if you expect huge yields from strains that normally do not give big yields, you are setting yourself up for disappointment. That means that you must choose a strain that will give you your expected yield.

LONG DAY PLANTS VS. SHORT DAY PLANTS

The next thing is to determine whether your strain of choice is a long day or short-day plant. If it is a short-day plant, then they require good amounts of darkness and short durations of exposure to light. On the other hand, long-day plants require long durations of light exposure and short periods of darkness.

You must understand this because every plant type requires unique feeding, environmental conditions, lighting, and hence do not mix well with others.

FLOWERING TIMES

This is one of the most important factors to consider when choosing a strain – especially for a beginner cannabis grower like you. Realize that certain plants take longer to flower compared to others. However, if you are not sure how long your plant's flowering period takes, the chances are that you will cut them too early or let them flower for too long and eventually underwhelm the harvest.

Checking the genetics of the plants is not just about the species of the plant you choose. Instead, it is about what state you receive the genetics. These two factors will help you start your plant life on the right track;

Seeds

Starting your garden the old-fashioned seeds-in-the-ground way, allows you to open the future to lots of benefits. For instance, seeds are known to be perfect for beginner growers. This is because they bring you closer to your plants to make a better grower once you know how things are done naturally.

The other thing you need to note is that seeds are the source of all genetics. It does not matter whether you create your strains or desire to hone in on new traits of a certain trait. The most important thing is that you must breed your plants. While seeds are not necessarily 100% pure during the start of your planting, they are very important when breeding and enhancing strains.

Additionally, when you start planting right from the seeds, you pave the way for more resilient plants. Bear in mind that the job of a clone is to grow an entire plant from one clipping. When you are working with clones, you are starting from a restoration stage – something that can be taxing if you go for the wrong clip. Simply start from seeds and ensure that you keep them well-maintained. This way, you end up with stronger plants.

Clones

When you work with clones, you get up and running as fast as possible. This is the reason most growers opt for clones instead of seeds. While seeds offer you stronger plants, the truth is that they cannot tell you the plant's sex until it is too late.

When working with clones, there is no need to pop seeds and waste them. If you pop the wrong seeds and then they don't grow or end up getting plants you did not want in the first place, clones will already be on their way to becoming full-grown plants. They are identical to the plants they were clones from, so you already know the plant's sex and whether or not it is what you want. This is how you make the best clones for your grow.

Therefore, if you are looking for a quick turn-around, clones are the way to go. The truth is, popping seeds and letting them grow can be very tricky, and even if clones are tricky too, rooting them can be done pretty fast.

How to differentiate female Marijuana from male plants

Male Cannabis

Male plants generate mainly pollen needed for the natural reproduction of cannabis plants; seeds appear when male plants are present in the mixture. You'll need a male plant if you want to produce your seeds. However, if you grow ordinary plants and want to pick flowers, we recommend getting rid of any males as soon as possible. You can't distinguish them from each other until they start to flower when the plants start revealing their sex.

"Balls" grow on male weeds, which are open to pollen release and eventually become like a small bouquet. Before this happens, you need to get rid of that road. If they succeed in releasing pollen, it will be too late. An explosion will take three weeks to complete. If you still don't know how to distinguish between them, male flowers don't have pestels at all.

Female Cannabis

Female plants are what everyone needs when growing cannabis, as they produce the kidneys that are part of the plant that contains the highest amount of THC. With just one male plant and a little pollen, your plants can end up filling their flowers with seeds. If you grow male and female plants in the same growing zone, the buds grown there will only produce seeds, so you cannot smoke them.

You can distinguish females because their flowers are not completely closed, they are quite open, and they have small hairs called pestels. They are incredibly easy to recognize because the first thing they produce is their pistils, which male plants do not have at all.

Hermaphrodite Cannabis

Hermaphrodites are a type of plant that includes both male and female flowers, so they will grow buds, but these buds and other plants will also be pollinated. Because of stress, plants may spontaneously become hermaphrodites or convert to them. This can roll over both female and male plants. Thai strains are more genetically prone to becoming hermaphrodites, though, with enough stress, any strain can rollover.

Many factors can cause stress in your plants and ultimately turn them around, such as extra light when they should be in the night cycle, too much or too little water, certain insects or pathogens, watering with cold water, or even a poorly done transplant. Hermaphrodites are not the best type of plants to store, as they can produce buds, but this is a risk because they can fertilize the rest of the plants.

It may seem confusing, but telling male and female weed plants apart is not hard; they are quite different. Planting regular seeds has its advantages. Feminization has its inconveniences; with feminized plants, you can get much bigger yields as you are guaranteed no male plants.

Although, remember that feminized seeds haven't been through a 100 percent natural process of becoming female, which can affect your weed's quality. This is why many cannabis connoisseurs have not yet made the leap from normal to feminized; they tend to reap slightly less yield, which is more potent and delicious.

BEST STRAINS FOR INDOOR GROWING

Now that you know how to choose the strain for you to grow, the next step is to choose the best strains in the market. One of the common questions I hear people asking all time is, "are all strains suitable for indoor grow?"

Well, the answer is YES!

The slightly longer version of this response is, yes, you can grow any strain you wish as long as you know that you can maintain them within the right conditions – climate, nutrition, space, and lighting, among others.

That said, the viability of all strains outdoors is quite a different story because of plant sensitivity. Most of the plants you would wish to plant outdoors may not stand the chill if you live in a colder climate for most of the year.

Beyond the climatic condition, there is also the issue of pests and diseases. In other words, if certain bugs find your plants outside so defenseless, then they are as good as gone! And even when you try to get rid of pests, your plants' quality will significantly decline.

So, what are the best strains for both indoor and outdoor grow – with conditions maintained constant as needed?

Strain #1 Critical

This is a perfect all-rounder, and I would recommend it mostly for outdoor growers aiming for extremely higher yields within a short flowering period. The good news is that the indoor growers can also plant them with a huge yield of approximately $600g/m^2$. They have strong narcotic stone because of about 18% THC levels and are said to be highly genetically stable – consisting of Skunk and Afghani genetics.

So, what makes it a great choice for indoor growers?

This is because it yields a higher harvest within a short flowering period of between 7 and 8 weeks. They are also vigorous and resilient with high-quality yields.

Royal Gorilla

This was once only available to smokers in the US. However, it has since crossed the pond allowing growers to enjoy all the amazing traits this strain has to offer. It is a clean split between two strains – Indica and Sativa. It has a THC content of between 24-27% offering users an impressive wave of cerebral relaxation.

Its taste finds roots in the forest and showcases its earthiness, pungent hits, and pine as it grows beautifully in the great outdoors. It takes about 9-10 weeks to flower. Once the flowering takes place, they give off hefty buds with bright green leaves. Because of their high resin content, they shine bright in the light and reach 90-160 com with an expected yield of between 500-550g/m^2.

With this strain, you are sure of a high-quality product.

Green Gelato

While most growers prefer starting with seeds, if you are looking for something to grow, you can go for the Green Gelato cultivars. It is a blend of Mint girl scout cookies and sunset sherbet. This combination is what makes this strain of cannabis salivating with a whopping THC content of 27%. It tastes like desserts with a perfect blend of citrusy and sweet notes with an earthy tone.

When growing this lady, you must regularly prune the plant using such techniques as fimming, topping into play, ScrOG, LST, or mainlining. Using this causes a clear high that is more physical, considering that there is slightly more Indica than Sativa in it.

Amnesia haze

This is one of the best strains with a flowering period of 10-11 weeks. The fact that you wait for a couple more weeks compared to other strains is accompanied by tremendous benefits as far as effects, potency, and flavor of the product is concerned. It has a THC content of 22% that is accompanied by haze freshness and a fruity flavor.

It has a powerful effect that feels like a parabolic flight into the stratosphere. This effect is accompanied by a rush of euphoria and a strong uplifting head high that makes you feel no effect of gravity whatsoever!

MEDICAL BENEFITS OF MARIJUANA

Humans who have cannabinoid receptors housed within their body which are prepared to bind with cannabinoids located in the Marijuana grow benefit from healing advantages for a range of illnesses. In reality, cannabinoid receptors are contained in humans before birth, and the ingredients are present in a mother's breast milk. Medical marijuana gains merit if you think about your body to be naturally tuned to interact with cannabinoids, and much more so if you acknowledge the increasing evidence of advantages to marijuana usage.

Digestion and Marijuana are no secret. Encountering "the munchies" is among the most apparent marijuana clichés. Regardless of the foolish connotation, studies suggest the endocannabinoid system helps modulate appetite. This is particularly good for the therapy of eating disorders. In reality, research published in the International Journal of Eating Disorders implied that cannabinoids might prove good at dealing with anorexia.

Pain Management

Chronic pain is among the most typical problems that make physicians prescribe medical Marijuana. A recently available survey published in the Spine Journal discovered that one out of five individuals in a Colorado spine facility had been using Marijuana to handle their pain. Of those who used it, nearly 90% said it moderately or greatly relieved their pain.

Mental Health

A typical misconception of Marijuana is the fact that it has detrimental effects on mental health. It's feasible that excessive doses of tetrahydrocannabinol (THC) could cause anxiety in certain individuals, as well as many who think it can expedite the beginning of predisposed personality problems. Still, these facts are yet to be established virtually by any respected studies.

The latest trend in the psychological health field has been investigating the human relationship with Marijuana. In turn, research has linked cannabinoids to a selection of psychological health concerns. The study catalog continues to be growing.

Not merely has Marijuana been associated with the brain wellbeing, cannabinoid receptor activity in mind before birth implies the compounds might be involved in mind growth. Marijuana was connected to the development of new neurons in the human brain, or maybe neurogenesis, and total brain plasticity.

Cancer treatment

It has long been recommended to fight the unwanted side effects of chemotherapy. Still, Oncologists throughout the planet are focusing on trials to find out if Marijuana may be utilized for treating cancer itself. Numerous individuals decide to grab the Rick Simpson Oil treatment program to remedy cancer, but there are lots of diverse techniques of going about the therapy.

What to Consider Before Trying Medical Marijuana

Constantly inform your doctor about any vitamins, dietary supplements, herbs, and over-the-counter medications you are using, including medical Marijuana. In case you reside in a state in which medical marijuana is legal, and would prefer talking to somebody who's effectively utilizing medical Marijuana for treating unwanted side effects of breast cancer, you must question your care team about linking you with an additional individual.

Insurance, Medicare, and Medicaid don't cover medical Marijuana. The price of medical Marijuana can start at approximately a hundred dollars per month and may be higher, depending on just how much is required. The main point here is the fact that medical Marijuana could be costly.

THC and CBD exist in levels that are different in various strains of Marijuana. THC, as well as CBD each, offer various benefits. For instance, CBD might be better at easing discomfort, while THC might be better at controlling nausea.

You'll probably need to perform a great deal of investigation by yourself to discover the ratio of CBD to THC that works ideal for managing your side effects. This could rather take a good deal of trial and error. What works for somebody else might not work for you.

You might need to visit many medical marijuana dispensaries until you come across one you are at ease with and possesses staff members who could respond to all your questions about the amounts of THC and CBD in the strains offered. Based on the laws in your state, some dispensaries might cater far more to recreational users than medical users. Health dispensaries are usually much more medical and also have staff members that are much more apt to get experience assisting individuals with cancer medical marijuana use for treating unwanted side effects.

It can be beneficial to contact the dispensary and explain the unwanted side effects you have, along with any experience you have had with Marijuana, and get if you could plan a consultation appointment and have a staff member. When you are at all uncomfortable, go to an alternative dispensary.

Several physicians who often recommend medical Marijuana recommend asking the dispensary team member several basic questions before you begin chatting specifically about your side effects:

- Is your Marijuana farmed using pesticides?
- Are your items stored and also handled correctly to stay away from contamination and spoilage?
- Are your products tested for bacteria and fungus? What exactly are the effects?
- Are your products tested for amounts of pesticides?
- What's your experience and training for recommending medical Marijuana?
- Perhaps, have you worked with cancer patients before?

Several oncologists have suggested that their patients attend a medical marijuana dispensary, instead of an outlet that caters to leisurely users. There's no study on if recreational Marijuana is as useful and safe for cancer patients as they are generally costlier healthcare grade range. However, several dispensaries take additional care to make sure there aren't any mold or pesticides in their medical-grade Marijuana.

If you work for the federal government, a federal government contractor, or maybe an employer that conducts frequent drug tests, you might face disciplinary action for utilizing medical Marijuana. Check your employer's medical marijuana policy before you begin making use of it.

In case you are a part of a clinical trial, there is a lot of unknown about how the ingredients in medical Marijuana might communicate with any experimental drugs. It will make great sense to speak with the physician coordinating the trial before you attempt any medical marijuana.

2

CHOOSE YOUR GROW ROOM/SPACE/GREENHOUSE

Once you figure out what strain you would like to plant and how you wish to start the garden, the next important thing is to determine where you would like to grow them in the first place.

Ask yourself whether you intend to buy a grow tent, build a greenhouse, or you are going to plant them on the ground outside. Do you intend to convert one of the rooms in the house into a grow room?

These questions are very important in ensuring that you have thoroughly thought of everything when getting the pots, clones, or seeds before getting started. However, before you delve into finding out the sort of housing you would like to plant your marijuana plants, it is important to reflect on the area of plants you intend to light – otherwise referred to as canopy of your growth.

To do this, you must follow these approaches;

HOW MUCH SPACE DO YOU WANT TO ALLOCATE FOR YOUR GROW ROOM?

If you want to know how big your garden is going to be, you must know the grow space limitations. Before going ahead to buy the bags of seeds or clones, take time to measure the grow area you wish to use in growing your marijuana plants. This way, you will have an idea of how many plants your space can hold.

HOW MANY PLANTS CAN YOU GROW IN THAT SPACE?

One good rule of thumb you must remember is that if you feel you are not sure how they grow buckets are going to be in the growing area, consider giving your plants at least 2-4 square feet in that space. Then divide that number by 2,3, and 4 to find out how many full-grown plants can grow there comfortably.

Ensure that the minimum you can go is at least 1 square foot. Try using a few buckets to measure it yourself.

Once you have measured out your grow space, and have an idea of what it will take to grow your garden, the next thing you should think about is how you plan to house them. There are three types of houses you can use for your plants;

Grow tents

This is one of the most common houses among indoor marijuana growers. They are not only increasingly convenient but also a manageable way of housing your plants. It does not matter whether you set it up in the garage or anywhere else in the house if you need a tent the size of a room, you can get it to accommodate all the plants you want to grow.

The good thing is that tents come in various sizes and styles for any grower and nearly all the plants you wish to plant. With a tent, there is no need to drill hanging hooks or vents for fans and lightings. What I like most about them is that you have superior control over the growing environment as opposed to many other setups.

Grow room

It does not matter whether you are going to set it up in the bedroom, closet, garage, or any other room in your apartment. The truth is that you can utilize your own space the way you see fit. Think of it as a much more convenient way of growing your plants than having to buy a tent.

With a grow room, you can get fresh air in fast and circulate it naturally throughout your garden.

One thing you must bear in mind is that grow rooms do not need one to purchase a whole tent. All you need to buy are reflective materials and fans to convert your room – something that is way cheaper than buying a tent. This also depends on the canopy you intend to grow.

Using grow rooms allow you to utilize the space that is already available to you. This includes windows with proper ventilation and power outlets. Trust me; there is not much to buy when converting a room into a grow room fit for your plants. The other thing is that once you have the right setting, you can use extra light from the sun to supplement the lights, especially when power is out.

Greenhouse

When doing indoor growing of your marijuana plants, you can consider using greenhouses when you don't have tons of room inside or outside either. You can think of either building or buying a greenhouse. The good thing with using a greenhouse is that you enjoy the same benefits as the outdoors – abundance of light and temperatures – with the added benefit of supplemental lighting and ventilation. When you grow crops in greenhouses, you not only save money on lighting by accessing the light from the sun, which is the optimal light source.

If you need more lighting, you can go for T5's or HID with lower power to back you up until the sun comes out whenever you have blackouts. You can also use plant training techniques such as light dep to get bigger plants from greenhouses. Because they are already acclimated to outdoor surroundings, you can take greenhouse plants out and plant outside. You don't need much training here.

3

CHOOSE YOUR MEDIUM

Once you know what strain you plan to grow and where you want it grown, then the next thing you must think about is the growth medium to use – which is the most important stage of preparation. The medium you choose to use will determine how many nutrients you need to include, the type of nutrients suited for your plants, how to feed your plants, and how to overcome challenging situations whenever they arise.

There are at least three popular grow mediums to choose from. Each grow medium has its advantages and disadvantages. That is why you must exercise caution to ensure that you make the right decision before growing your plants.

SOIL

This is one of the most used all-purpose mediums that is perfect for the growing of marijuana plants. The good thing with using soil as a growing medium is that it does not need much supplemental nutrition considering that they are already loaded with high-quality nutrients.

If you consider mixing your super soil, you end up eliminating about 90% of supplemental nutrients. Soil is already loaded with the nutrients you need for your plant's life.

Soil is great for beginners because it has a lot of buffer room about readings and feedings. It retails nutrients that are best for all mediums. Your plants need little nutrients when they are just starting to grow, and when they need more, you just need to add a little.

That said, growing your plants in the soil means that they

are generally going to take longer to grow. Additionally, if the soil has nutrient issues, they might not show up immediately, and when they do, it can be hard to fix them. The truth is, your plants risk getting so sick in the soil beyond repair when there is an issue there, and you don't know what it is.

Unlike the hydroponic systems where the whole plant roots hang down in a bucket, roots in the soil go all over the place, and when you don't have enough room for them, you end up with root-bound plants – and those are not good at all!

Getting the Soil Right

Anyone who has tried any type of gardening will understand the importance of getting the soil conditions right. The soil is where your plant will gather the necessary nutrients to grow. There are also different types of soil; texture and drainage can make a huge difference.

Good soil for your marijuana plant will have a light texture and be fairly good at retaining water. If the soil is heavy, the plant roots will struggle to spread, and there will be too much water for the healthy development of the plant.

Generally, it is not advisable to simply go outside and dig some of your soil; it will probably not be beneficial for your marijuana plant. Instead, you should look at purchasing a potting soil. This is soil that has been specially formulated to provide young plants with all the nutrients they need to get them started using this **feeding schedule.**

Some of the ingredients you could have in your soil include;

Perlite - This is a common addition to soil and one that you could easily add to a standard bag of soil purchased in your local garden center. It looks like little white rocks, and it will increase water's ability to drain through your soil, preventing you from overwatering your plant. Also, it encourages oxygen into the soil for your plants. However, you shouldn't use too much of this if you are planning to add nutrients to your soil; keep it to 10% of your soil mix.

Bone Meal - A bone meal is high in phosphorous and calcium, which are great for your plants as they start to flower. However, it a slow-releasing fertilizer, so it's best to be mixed in your soil when you start potting. The nutrients will then be available when they are ready to flower.

Composted Humus - This is any type of compost that has naturally decomposed. Because natural materials have been broken down, it is full of nutrients that will benefit your plants.

It also benefits your plant by helping the soil to retain moisture and oxygen. The result is better quality soil for your plants.

Bat Guano - This is a great way to add nutrients to your soil. Simply sprinkle it on the top of the soil and keep it moist. This will encourage bacteria to feed on the guano and break it down to create the nutrients your plants need. It can be used throughout the entire growing cycle.

Vermiculite - This is a good addition if you are losing water too quickly in your plants. A little will help to slow down the drainage and can make the soil heavier. But it will also restrict the addition of oxygen to the soil.

Worm Castings - These are full of nutrition that is essential and extremely beneficial to your marijuana plants. There are no real downsides to adding this to your soil. It can make a valuable addition regularly to encourage good microbes and provide nutrients for your growing plants.

Pumice - Pumice is a type of volcanic rock. Because it is porous, it is good at holding water and allowing airflow. It works similarly to perlite and should be mixed with your soil.

Kelp - Kelp is a plant in itself and, as such, contains all the nutrients that every plant needs to survive. This makes it a great addition to your soil for encouraging plant growth.

It is also extremely beneficial as it is excellent at repelling slugs and other pests from your Marijuana while keeping the soil moist. You can cover your soil throughout the growth of your plant, but only after it has germinated, you don't want to suffocate it as well as the weeds!

Once you have got your soil sorted, you now need to consider fertilizers. If you plan on repotting your plants regularly, this might not be necessary as the fresh soil will have its nutrients. But, if this is not the case, fertilizers are essential to ensure your plants have everything they need to grow big and strong!

It is possible to mix your fertilizers. However, unless you are certain about what is already in your soil, this can be a dangerous process. Homemade fertilizers can react with chemicals in the soil and cause a detrimental effect on your plant.

As a beginner, you should purchase one of the many fertilizers on the market. This will help you to choose the right one for the stage of plant growth. A general fertilizer works well for seedlings, but flowering plants must have balanced nutrition.

Once you know your soil types and understand your plants' needs, you can use the following as your fertilizer:

Chicken Manure - A little chicken manure can go a long way when looking after your plants; it's full of nutrients essential for all stages of plant growth.

Vinegar - Did you know that one drop of white vinegar on baking soda will release carbon dioxide, which your plants thrive on.

A good way of doing this is to put the vinegar in a plastic bag and hang it over the bowl. Prick a tiny hole to allow it to drip out slowly. But, you must do this in a way that keeps the carbon dioxide in the space; this is not good for outside growing. There will also be a heavy smell of vinegar that you won't want others noticing.

Kitchen Waste - All the organic food waste you usually chuck away can be put into a pile to encourage them to decompose. Once they start to decompose, you can put them on the top layer of your soil, releasing all the nutrients your plant needs when you are watering them.

HYDROPONICS

This is an all-water growing medium. It is soil-less, less messy, and whenever you run into nutrient issues, you can fix them faster and easily as opposed to when your plans are grown in soil mediums. The good thing about this growing medium is that it takes less time than soil plants to be harvested.

Growing Marijuana in hydroponics ensures that your plants absorb nutrients faster and grow faster than grown in soil or coco. However, this requires someone who is already advanced to a professional grower.

That said, there is no buffer when growing your marijuana plants in hydroponics. With hydroponic systems, just a single misstep and your plants will feel it. While nutrient issues are much easier to fix, the problem is that you are likely to get more nutrient spikes than you would in soil.

Considering that your plants are essentially in the water at the root level, the basins and water must be checked regularly to prevent the growth of fungus, mold, or root rot that are damaging to the whole plant.

COCO

Think of coco as the perfect middle ground between soil and hydroponics. Even though there is no nutritional value to using coco in growing your plants, however, just like soil, the nutrients added tend to be held longer than when you use hydroponics. This simply means that there is no need to run heavy water flow like you would in a hydro system.

The good thing with coco as a growing medium is that your plants are assured of getting nutrients from the beginning rather than choosing to trust that soil is good enough to carry your plants through to the flowering phase.

Cocos retain nutrients better than hydro systems. However, they don't hold the nutrients longer than soil mediums. The plants take longer to grow compared to the hydro system, but they tend to grow faster than when you are using soil mediums. Using coco coir as your grow medium requires your skill level to be advanced or professional.

What you must note is that the nutrient issues here can be tricky to address because of the semi- retainability of the medium. Here, you also don't have a ton of buffer. Finally, if you fail to break down and mix your coco well, the pH might spike, causing harm to your plants.

4

CHOOSE YOUR GROW LIGHTS

At this point, we are almost through with the vitals of what you require to get started growing your plants. You can take a deep breath because we are almost ready to grow our marijuana plants!

Now, once you are through with this stage, the next thing would be to grab your tools and get down to work – literally. However, before we get down to the easy stuff, we might want to figure out one last thing – the lighting system for growing your plants. This is one of the last things that will determine your yield, the complexity of growing, and the amount of energy your plants will need during growth.

Like most things in your grow room, all kinds of lights you intend to use, have their advantages and disadvantages. Some add a ton of heat to the growing space, while others don't even give enough power. Others even have too much power without necessarily adding to a degree of temperature to the grow surroundings.

Before you decide to use it to grow your plants, you must take time to understand the benefits and challenges of every lighting option in the market. Here are some of the options and their pros and cons;

HIGH-INTENSITY DISCHARGE (HID) GROW LIGHTS

I love most about the HID because they offer the closest light spectrum to that of the sun. This way, your marijuana plants get the kind of lighting they need for their growth. With this kind of lighting, you are assured of healthy plants right from the beginning to the time when you harvest a huge yield – especially when you take the time to train properly.

They also come in a wide range of reflectors and wattages that suit your growing needs. In short, there is an HID for any application you wish to use it for.

If you just need the lights for standard to grow, then a regular HPS/MH will work perfectly for you. However, if your plants are spaced differently, here is what you can work with;

- 400 watts Grow lights are perfect for 1-3 plants within a 3x3 ft or 2x4 ft of each other.

- 600 watts Grow lights are perfect for 3-4 plants in a 4x4 or 5x5 feet each other.
- 1000 watts are strongest of all the grow lights in this category and can grow between 5 and 6 plants within 6x6 feet grow area.

That said, it is important to note that double-ended grow lights are much more intense than standard, single-ended bulbs. This is mainly because of the dual base connection they offer, hence firing from two connections instead of one at the base of the bulb.

CMH grow lights, on the other hand, offer an even spectrum of lights without excess red or blue light spectrums. They have ceramic bases that make them more superior to DE lights with similar wattages. Additionally, they can fire at high wattages.

LED GROW LIGHTS

You must bear in mind that giving your plants the exact spectrum of light they need for their growth. LEDs are one of the most incredible ways to give your plants the light they require without necessarily exposing them to excess heat or light spectrums they do not need.

They can pinpoint the precise wavelengths of light your marijuana plants absorb and offer them exactly that. In other words, there is nothing your marijuana plants will waste with LED lights compared to HIDs.

While the yield you get from plants when using LED lights is not as much as you harvest from HIDs, the truth is that LEDs go a long way toward helping your plants give a superior flavor. The product you get is stickier and of high quality too.

Trust me, with LEDs; your marijuana plants will give you properties other grow lights may not give – like IR and UV for resins. The light generated has an intense wavelength. This means that if you move them too close to the plants, you risk bleaching your marijuana plants.

For marijuana plants, Advance Spectrum Max engineer the perfect spectrum for them. Using supplemental grow lights offers you limited spectrum range – either all blue, all red, dual, or a triband. However, if you choose to use LEDs, they will fill the gaps your main lights do not have. Full-spectrum LED grow lights; on the other hand, offer your marijuana plants a wide light spectrum covering all the spectrums your plants will need. The only challenge with HIDs is that they give plants too many spectrums to process – eventually, the plants end up wasting.

LEDs tend to outperform the HIDs in terms of quality – even if they have the same wattage. For instance, if you have a 600 watts LED, it will outperform a 600 Watts HID with a similar spectrum output because of the wide spectrum LEDs give.

T5 GROW LIGHTS

With these kinds of lights, you get a limited amount of heat. They are much similar to the HIDs because they both have "grow" and "bloom" spectrums and so much more. Even though they have limited power and lower-yielding harvests, they are perfect alternatives for marijuana growers who wish to grow their plants without using up too much energy or bleaching the plants as LEDs do.

The good thing with these grow lights is that you can use them to grow close to anything. However, considering that they are not that strong, your plants will remain small. According to research, they run 75% cooler compared to HIDs. The yields, in this case, are small but will get you a pinch of yield at the end of the growing period.

They come in a wide range of sizes hence covering the canopy you wish to grow pretty well. It good when you are growing marijuana, clones, spices, and herbs.

5

TOOLS

Throughout your growing experience, you are going to use lots of tools from scissors, meters, controllers, to gloves, among others. Trust me; there are lots of tools that will make your time in the grow space. While all these tools play important roles in growing your Marijuana and giving you the yields, you have always wanted, some of them are more important than others.

Here are key tools you will need even before you start setting up your grow space;

HYGROMETER

A wide range knows this tool of names, but it is critical for growing your marijuana plants. They help you read the temperatures of your growing space and the level of CO_2

and humidity in your space. When growing Marijuana indoors, one of the most important things is to be keen on the growing environment.

You will feel how humid or hot the surroundings are, but a hygrometer will tell you precisely what is happening in your marijuana garden. When the conditions are out of range, you can easily and promptly adjust as necessary so that your plants have optimal growth conditions.

PRUNING SHEARS

This is another important tool that will help you take off drying leaves, train your plants, and clipping new clones. Trust me; you will be surprised how important and handy shears can be. They will help you clean cut off your plants, a very important process for the whole plant.

When the plant leaves are not removed as required, it can cause unnecessary damage to the whole plant. Unnecessary damage translates to the plant sending out signals to the rest of the plant sections for healing, hence hindering growth. That also has an impact on the final yield you get.

PH/PPM METERS

It does not matter what growing medium you are using for your growth. What matters most is that you know the pH level of the nutrient-rich water you are using to feed your plants. This ensures that you are not poisoning your plants at all. PPM – also referred to in full as parts per million – are very important, and you must keep an eye on them to ensure that your marijuana plants are not eating too much or too little.

MICROSCOPE

You may be thinking, "isn't this for a research lab?" Well, think of your garden as a lab in itself. When you are growing your marijuana plants, you are researching some sort at different plant growth stages. At one point, you want to know the sex of the plants, the trichomes, and searching for bugs – and what better tool to use than a microscope.

Microscopes will help you spot tiny details or features of your plants every step of the way to ensure that you are on the right track with your growth.

HEAT THERMOMETER

It is always a brilliant idea to know how much heat is in your canopy. However, you cannot know the exact temperature readings if you don't have a thermometer. This is precisely why you must consider investing in a good heat thermometer that can help you read the temperatures of a specific surface or surfaces that are not easy to measure.

6

DAILY MAINTENANCE

I t does not matter whether you are growing your plants indoors or outdoors because each day in the garden presents its unique challenges. There are times when the pH and PPM levels spike or the temperatures go out of range – and let us not get started in the pests!

Making the initial investment in growing cannabis is always helpful for growers who have already faced the same issues you might be facing during your first growing experience. Before we proceed, it is important to take note of some of the common mistakes you should avoid;

Overfeeding: It is best to follow the directions provided by the manufacturer.

Overwatering medium-based plants: If you have decided to use buckets/pots for your plants, you will need to use a hefting approach. That is when you judge its weight by 'hefting.' First, you want to judge its dry weight—via hefting. Water, the plant until the water, is running through the drain holes —heft again. When the pot feels the same wet as it did dry, it is time to water again. It is basic common sense.

Over-Analyzing: Watching the 'weed' grow is similar to watching a first-born child. You don't want to miss a single thing. However, don't try to fix every yellow leaf you see; watch out for the big ones.

Overspending on Materials: If you are a beginner, try to stay on a set budget. It is easy to get 'caught up' in the excitement of it all.

CHECK PH LEVELS

If you are working with a hydroponic system, the most important thing is to calibrate your pH meter and the meter used in measuring the water levels in the reservoir. If you are using coco and soil as your grow mediums, ensure that you water your plants. Regularly check the runoff pH levels to ensure that they are optimal as low levels are toxic to the plant and too high lowers the growth of your plants.

This is why you must have a perfect acidity level in the water you have in the reservoirs – something between 5.5 and 6.0. If you don't check the pH and it is too high, your plants will not grow as you want them to. Simply use pH downs to bring it back to optimal levels. If the pH is too low, on the other hand, try to regulate it to optimal levels.

Here's how your plants are affected by the pH levels;

- Less or equal to 3.5 – causes plant root damage
- 4.0-4.5 – causes poor nutrient uptake by the plant roots
- 5.0-5.4 – optimal pH level for optimal growth of your marijuana plants
- 5.4-5.8 – also perfect pH levels for your plant growth
- 6.0-7.0 – is acceptable pH levels but you must be keen to ensure that they don't go higher than this leads to poor nutrient uptake by the plant
- 8.5 and above – cause root damage to the plant and decreased growth.

CHECK PPM LEVELS

This is an important element that gives you an idea of how many elements are available for the plants' feeding solution. It is an important factor to keep an eye on ensuring that you are not overfeeding your plants with too many nutrients.

When your plants are young, you don't need to give them too many nutrients because they do not need it. In that case, they could use between 100-250 ppm.

During the first half of the vegging cycle of the plants, ensure that the ppm levels are between 300 and 400. This stage comes right after you transplant the seedlings, and at this point, your plants still do not need too many nutrients.

During the second half of vegging, you must keep the nutrient levels at 450 to 700 ppm. Here, your plants have started needing more nutrients than the first two stages.

During the first half of the flowering stage, ensure that the nutrients are between 750 and 950 ppm. At this stage, your marijuana plants are eating more food because they are actively growing.

During the second half of flowering, they will need even more foods than before and hence the reason to keep the nutrient levels between 1000 and 1600 ppm.

As the flowering stage ends and you get into the harvest season, ensure that the levels are close to 0 as possible. You must flush your plants so that there are no more particles left over.

CHECK GROWS FOR PESTS.

One thing you must remember at all times is that your garden is a pest's grocery store. This means that you must check your plants at least once to ensure that pests are not feasting on your growth. Ensure that you check both the tops and bottoms of the leaves, walls, floors, as well as buckets and grow mediums for pests, fungus, and mold build-up.

This is especially important for your marijuana plants outside and in greenhouses, considering that they are exposed to more pests, fungi, and molds than those growing indoors. Most of the outdoor plants are at risk of rats and rabbits, fungal spores, and high amounts of mold, among other pests.

INSPECT LEAVES FOR SIGNS OF NUTRIENT DEFICIENCIES

When your grow is not getting the right amount of nutrients they require for growth and nourishment, the truth is that they will not get you the yield you need at the end of the harvest season. If your grow space is free of pests, but your plant's leaves are turning yellow/brown, curling, and becoming brittle, the chances are that they are experiencing a deficiency in their nutrition.

Ensure that you check the color of your plant leaves at least once a day. This way, you can easily catch a problem if there is one. Pay close attention to their deficiency charts and nutrient bottles to find out if there are issues. If you find nutrient issues, be sure to supplement your marijuana plants with the missing nutrient or elements needed.

CHECK ENVIRONMENTAL CONDITIONS

Some of the essential environmental conditions for your grow include humidity, temperatures, and CO2 levels. These are the most important factors to keep a close eye on every day because they affect transpiration and photosynthesis processes.

When the lights are off, the acceptable temperature drop should be within 10-15º F. If it is above this, then you know that there is a problem and must be addressed immediately. Here are the correct conditions for every stage of your grow;

- Seedlings and clones – 72-82 º F at a humidity of between 70 and 75%
- Vegging stage – 68-78 º F at a humidity of between 50 and 70%
- Flowering stage – 68-77 º F at a humidity of between 40 and 50%
- Harvest stage – 65-75 º F at a humidity of between 45 and 55%

At this stage, things should be starting to come together. You've chosen the type of Marijuana you wish to grow, pot size, and the type of system you wish to use to grow your Marijuana. For clarity, if you are a beginner, then it is best to start with a pot, good quality soil and some fertilizer. Providing you've chosen the right light set up and understand the light cycles, you're nearly ready to start planting.

First, you need to understand the importance of getting the humidity right, ventilate your crop, and perhaps the most concerning of all, how to prevent Marijuana's aroma penetrating the air. Even if you have just six plants, this aroma might be enough to attract others that would like your crop for their reasons!

You are probably already aware that humidity simply refers to the amount of moisture present in the air. The more there is, the more humid the air.

The marijuana plant is not keen on high levels of moisture; this is good as modern heating systems tend to dry the air in your home. However, nature is all about balance. Low humidity levels equate to high evaporation pressure. This is good as it helps your plants to absorb vital nutrients. However, if the humidity becomes too low, then the plant will assume there is a problem with water and protect itself from dehydration.

Unfortunately, this means it will no longer absorb water and will not be able to grow!

The temperature of your grow room partly controls humidity. It is, therefore, essential to have a humidity meter and consistently monitor it; this will ensure you can react appropriately if the humidity levels change.

You need to know the current humidity rating. It's best to use a hygrometer for this (analog or digital). It is worth noting that the humidity is affected by the temperature outside the house. For instance, temperatures outside below 15° Fahrenheit your humidity reading will probably be about

35%. It should increase by 5% every time the temperature rises by 10°F.

Air-conditioning or a dehumidifier. These are a great way of removing moisture from a room, allowing you to bring it down to the most appropriate level for your needs. Cat litter can be your best friend if the humidity gets too high. Simply spread some in a tray and leave it in the growing room. It attracts moisture and will lower the moisture level in the room.

Add moisture by having water in the room in open bowls; it will evaporate into the room, increasing the humidity levels. Another option is to use a humidifier that will push moisture into your room, helping to boost the moisture level.

You can also use a vaporizer; this uses warm water and vaporizes it into the air, boosting the moisture content, if needed.

Add ventilation; this can reduce the humidity level if the outside air already has a lower humidity rating. A fan, coupled with an atmospheric controller, can make a huge difference to the ease in which you can control the humidity levels. De-leaf some of the plants with the most leaves on. Excessive leaves can increase the humidity in your growing room; this is particularly true when you have limited airflow.

These are all great methods to boost or decrease your moisture levels. However, the key to this approach is making sure that you monitor the levels regularly and adjust them slowly.

Unsurprisingly getting the humidity wrong will affect the growth rate of your plants. But this is not the only sign that there is an issue with humidity:

White powder - This is a fungal disease that only arrives when the atmosphere is too humid. A good airflow system can help to prevent this.

Bud Rot - If your buds' insides are white or brown with mold, then you have bud rot, and your crop is effectively useless. This is incredibly frustrating, and not something that will be an issue if you monitor the humidity rating properly.

Nutrition - If your plants start to look like they have yellow or burnt tips, they are more effectively consuming more water than they should be; this is usually because of low humidity.

Increase the humidity levels immediately. Remember, the right humidity levels will encourage maximum growth!

Choosing the Right Ventilation System

Ventilation is often a difficult issue. The basic truth is that no matter how many or how few plants you are growing, you are likely to be growing them in confined conditions.

There is a good reason for this; you don't want everyone knowing what you are doing. Even when growing them for medical reasons, many people do not realize this is an option and are likely to report you. This will give you unnecessary hassle and highlight to others that you have Marijuana.

You need ventilation for several reasons:

Toxin removal - Marijuana is no different from most plants in that it pushes toxins out of itself through the leaves. Airflow helps to remove these toxins from the plants. Without this, they can stay there, preventing the plant from pushing more out and even encouraging the growth of mold.

Humidity- We already looked at humidity and understood the importance of getting this right. However, as we mentioned, airflow can help with distributing the same humidity level across the room.

A fan can simply move air around your room, helping to decrease the chance of mold forming on your plants. It can also be used to bring air inside from outside the building; this can lower the temperature to reduce the humidity levels. This approach is especially effective if you add a temperature and humidity control device as the fan can switch automatically.

Creating the Ventilation

The most comprehensive method of creating ventilation is through the use of several items:

- An intake fan, this sucks air in from the outside.
- An extractor fan; pushes the air out of your grow room and into the outside world.
- An interior fan moves air across the plants. This might not be necessary if you only have a few plants.

- Some sort of air filter device.

The intake fan does more than just bring air in; it pushes it in at the same rate the extractor is removing it; this allows the air pressure to remain the same, preventing any disruption to the growing cycle of the plants.

CHECK FILTERS IN YOUR GROW ROOMS.

The other daily maintenance, you must pay attention to the filters around the grow space – especially if you are growing your marijuana plants indoors. This way, you ensure that your plants can grow in a clean space free of dust, clogging their stoma. On the other hand, your filter will ensure that you can hide smells from your grow area.

You must note that if you can smell your grow from 3 feet away from the filter or have dust built up in your grow space, the chances are that your plants need an inspection, repair, and a change of filters for a clean one.

Dealing with the aroma

Of course, if you've ever had any experience with growing Marijuana, you'll know it has a distinctive smell, which is relatively easy for others to detect. While ventilation is essential, this will push the plant's smell into your house, not something you are likely to want to risk!

First, you need a fan to remove the air. You should already

have this as part of your airflow and humidity control measures. Moving the air outside will reduce the potency of the aroma from your marijuana plants.

But this is not enough; the aroma could still give you away and attract unwanted attention. There are several ways of dealing with the aroma:

Carbon Filter - This is the perfect addition to your extractor fan. All the air leaving your room should be pulled through the fan. In the process, it will need to pass through the carbon filter you have fitted.

Choose a filter that fits perfectly into your exhaust ventilation system (there are sets). The carbon will attract the aroma and hold it, preventing it from getting into the outside world. You do need to have a fan, and you need a quality carbon filter to do the job properly. Searching on eBay or Amazon for a "carbon filter fan" will do the job.

Negative Ions - A more advanced method is to use a negative ion generator. These charges the particles in the air and effectively gives these particles the ability to neutralize the odor in other particles, eliminating the Marijuana's aroma.

A carbon filter is more effective, but this is a great alternative.

HEPA - This is an alternative type of filter that can be used in your grow room. However, it still requires airflow through it. The fan does not need to ventilate outside the grow room, making it an attractive option in some scenarios.

Choose the ventilation system and aroma protection system that suits your needs and budget. This will ensure you monitor the humidity, and your plants will start growing well. It is worth noting that a HEPA filter cannot filter very small particles. You will need a carbon filter for this.

CHECK THE SURFACE FOR EXCESS MOISTURE.

This is often a sign of temperature issues and humidity as well. It could also indicate that there is a problem in the airflow and CO2 problems.

You must note that excess moisture in the grow area risk your plants of mold and serves as a good breeding ground for harmful bacteria, which will ultimately destroy your plants. If you check your growing areas – basins, reflectors, buckets, and reservoirs, among others – and find out that there is excess moisture, ensure that you completely dry it.

If you are growing your marijuana plant in soil, it is a brilliant idea to check the moisture levels of the soil to ensure that you are feeding the plants as required. Simply stick your finger about ½" to 1" to check for dryness of moisture. Alternatively, you can use a moisture meter. If using cocoa, you can also check for moisture levels the same way.

However, if your grow is in hydroponics, you don't need to

measure the moisture content considering your plant is in the water anyways. The best thing is to ensure that your plants are getting sufficient amounts of water. Ensure that the water is not rolling right off the pebbles and Rockwool, leaving your plants dry. At the same time, you must not overpower your plants with water, as this might result in a nutrient lockout.

CHECK THE HEIGHT OF YOUR LIGHTS ABOVE YOUR PLANTS.

You must ensure that the height of your lights is not too close or too far from the plants. Remember what we discussed earlier – not all lights are the same – HID, LEDs, and T5 fluorescent grow lights. All these require different heights.

For instance, if you are using;

HID grow lights

- 1000 watts lights must be between 16-31" from the plants
- 600 watts lights must be positioned 14-25" from the plants
- 400 watts lights must be positioned 12-19" from the plants

T5 fluorescent grows lights must be positioned 5-12" above the plants.

LED grow lights

- 900 watts and above must be positioned 26-42" from a vegging plant
- 600-850 watts lights must be positioned 24-26" from a vegging plant
- 450-550 watts lights must be placed 20-30" away from a vegging plant
- 240-400 watts lights must be 16-30" away from a vegging plant.

That said, you must measure the canopy temperatures to ensure that you don't end up burning your plants or underwhelming plant leaves. The canopy temperatures must be the same throughout you grow space.

7

PRE-VEGGING STAGE

At this point, you are now ready and have the genetics ready to hit the ground. Before you get right to it – the vegging stage – it is important that you get your seeds or clones ready for your future harvest. This is what we refer to as the pre-vegging stage.

How then can you start your Grow from Seeds and Clones?

Once you have your seeds and clippings ready, the first thing is to get them into a growing medium so that they can get started on a healthy journey. You must bear in mind that this stage is where you make or break your seeds/clones. If you get them started on the wrong footing, the chances are that you will pay for it later. This is why you must start your seeds or clones on the right footing for the seedlings' quality when the time comes for transplanting into larger pots.

What happens if you are starting with seeds?

Growing your marijuana plants from seeds is mostly a natural way of starting a garden. However, it is also the most challenging.

One thing you must note is that when seeds start their lives as plants, their taproots come out of the seeds and pops the shell. This allows the roots to penetrate the medium for nutrition. The good thing is that you don't have to use special seeds to grow like you would clones.

There are at least three ways you can do propagation before they get into the vegging stage;

POPPING SEEDS ON PAPER TOWELS

Here, when you pop seeds on moist paper towels, you know whether you have tap grassroots rather than playing the waiting game for your seedlings to finally show up. All you need is to plant the popped seeds in your growth medium, and you are ready to go!

STARTING IN CELLS

Note that, regardless of whether the seeds are popped or not, you can start your plants in starter cells or plastic cups that are filled with your grow medium – like soil or coco.

I love most about starter cells because they have everything you need to get your seeds to grow into seedlings with a medium that supports the proper growth of roots. If you have a humidity dome, you can easily propagate more than a single seedling at a time.

You may be thinking, "how do plastic cups work in this case?" Well, they work the same way only that in this case, you offer your seeds more room for root growth as opposed to the case of starter cells. This way, you get a chance to start your grow with larger plants. The most important thing is that you exercise caution not to allow the plants to grow too large in plastic cups as this might cause them to be root-bound, which is never good for young plants.

STARTING IN POTS, YOU WILL BE USING.

If you don't wish to pre-pop your seeds before transplanting them to their designated grow areas, you can place them directly into plant pots you intend to use for the plant's entire life.

While this will take the hassle of transplanting off your plate, the truth is that you stand the risk of overwhelming your plants with excess light and water than they need. On the other hand, if you choose to plant them directly into large pots, you must consider feeding them minimally and offering them light softly.

What if you choose to start with clones instead of seeds?

Remember, starting your marijuana plants from clones is a surefire way of ensuring that the plant genetics you are interested in growing is intact and precisely what you are looking for. With seeds, you risk growing your plants only to later realize that they are not the ones you wanted. While seeds can grow stronger than clones, the truth is that they can be a toss-up.

Your seeds can either be female or male, and even though they are the sex you are looking for, the truth is that you cannot guarantee they possess strain traits you are after. Clones, on the other hand, are derived from the plants you are looking for.

If you intend to replicate the genes to the tee, you must start from clones. Use a sterile scalpel and identify healthy fan leaves to cut from the branch at least at a 90° angle. Once you have the clippings, place them in water to avoid bubbles from entering the plant stem.

You can also use clipping gels on the clippings you took from the mother plants. Then insert the clones in starter cells and cover them with a humidity dome. Realize that standard starter cells are perfect for transplanting growing clones in coco or soil mediums. If you can, use Rockwool starter cells if you intend on using hydroponics as your grow medium because they are great for transplanting clones.

Ensure that the surroundings are humid enough – approximately 72-77° F – at least for two weeks. Once they get to the desired size, you are looking for, transplant following **these guidelines;**

8

TRANSPLANTING YOUR SEEDLINGS AND CLONES

Once you have your seedlings and clones as big as you would like them to be, you are ready for transplanting your marijuana plants into permanent pots for the rest of the life. One thing you must bear in mind is that marijuana plants hate jumping around from one bucket to the other. This is why it is necessary to keep transplanting to the minimum. The best way to do this is if you learn the appropriate pot size you wish the plants to end up in.

I will reiterate – keep transplanting to the minimum!

It should be between 1-2 transplants at most. Anything more than this might risk the plants suffering severe damage.

AVOIDING TRANSPLANT SHOCK

Have you ever taken a plant out of a container and put them on the ground or in another container?

When you move the plants from their original home to another, you expose them to a risk of deformation. Regardless of whether these deformations come in the form of limp, slow growth, dries up, or halted growth, these outcomes result from the direct consequences of extreme environmental changes.

The change here is – being uprooted!

Well, you might be thinking, "if transplanting damages the plant, what else can we do?"

Don't worry – just because your plants suffer transplant shock does not mean that they will eventually die. This means that you have to treat your seedlings like babies until they get back in shape. At this stage, they are very delicate, and depending on how severe the shock was will determine the length of recovery they will need before they spring back to normal.

To avoid shocking your plants too much during transplanting, try to pay attention to these directions;

Don't mess with the plant roots.

When transplanting, it is almost impossible not to disturb the roots. However, the most important thing you need to do here is to avoid digging into the plant area to lower the chances of damaging the plant roots. The best way to go about this is to try as much as you can to go around the entire medium and into the new pot by simply turning the pot or cell over as soon as the medium is compacted. This way, you can take the whole thing and move it into the new medium.

Avoid disturbing the root ball.

You must avoid shaking the soil or breaking the Rockwool in which your plants are in. This way, you ensure that the main root ball is intact.

Offer your plants plenty of water during transplanting.

Realize that nothing will shock your plants more than not giving it water. The truth is that when transplanting your plants, they will mostly be in recovery mode once they get out of the first medium. This is why you must ensure that when they need food, they can access it.

Ensure that the root balls are kept moist at all times. If not, the roots will dry and become damaged. Don't get me wrong – I am not saying that you should overwater your plants. Instead, you must watch them closely so that you can feed them when they need it.

KNOWING WHEN TO TRANSPLANT

This is one of the most important factors when it comes to transplanting. Yes, you may already know what transplanting is all about and what it is for, but if you don't know when to do it, then the chances are that your plants will live in their initial pots for eternity. When you cannot tell by just looking at the height of the plant, here are a few pointers on when the right to transplant comes;

Growing in starter cells

If your plants are in starter cells, simply feel around the root zone. If the medium is loose and there are not many roots, maintain them in their starter cells. However, if the medium is hardened around the root zone and the roots are good, then your plants are ready to get out of their initial home into the next.

Growing in soil

If you are growing your marijuana plants in large pots you wish to use for the rest of their life, then all you have to do is let your plants grow. However, if you started them in plastic cups with soil, ensure that your plants have rooted. The plants should not be root-bound if the soil is hardened but not compact, tip over the cup, and move the whole of it to a new bucket.

Growing in Rockwool cubes

It is important that the plant roots, in this case, are plentiful but not so few that transplanting will cause them damage. Rockwool is often used in coco and hydroponic mediums. In these two growth mediums, even a few roots would overload the plants with nutrients once transplanted.

PREPPING THE MEDIUM

Before getting your plants into the grow medium, ensure that it will not shock your plants any further. Well, this part is pretty easy if you are very careful. If you are planting them in soil, prepping the soil is easy because you need to add perlite to it and then gently water it. Then properly mix the elements very well to create super soil.

If you intend to plant them in coco coir, realize that the coco husks are neutral in pH. This means that you don't need to prep the medium other than breaking it down. This is usually in block form. Simply soak it and break it up and then fill a bucket with it. After that, soak the whole medium in the best nutrient solution of choice.

If you are using hydroponics, simply add a little seaweed extract into your medium. You could also add in shock treatment before you transplant your plants. Ensure that the temperature of both the water and nutrient solutions is at 68° F or room temperature. This ensures that you don't end up shocking the roots. Then load the water with a nutrient solution. Here are some of the best hydroponic mediums available for your indoor marijuana needs.

PREPPING NUTRIENTS

One more thing to go over before placing your plants in their permanent homes – the nutrient prep. How you mix your nutrients into your feeding solution is key to a successful transplant. This, too, is pretty easy. You must prep your water and mix all your nutrients and its elements well before you feed them to the plants.

Start by testing the pH and ppm levels of your water to ensure that they are optimal for healthy plants. If some reason your water is hard or feels too loaded with trace elements, simply run them through a reverse osmosis system to clean it up.

If you cannot use reverse osmosis systems, allow the water to sit out in open air for a while for the chlorine to be taken out. Aerate your water by hand or using a pump to ensure that there is sufficient oxygen for it to be beneficial to the plants.

Pay attention to the nutrients and the manufacturer's dosage recommendation. While some growers consider using half the recommended dosage by the manufacturer, you must base it on strength. Find the recommended dosage amount on the feeding chart that accompanied the nutrients. Then take the size of the reservoir or water canteen – if using soil or coco mediums – to determine how many mL of nutrients you will need.

Let us consider an example where your reservoir is 10 gallons – which roughly translates to about 38 liters – and your nutrients call for 5 mL of a given nutrient per gallon. In this case, you are going to mix 50 mL into your reservoir.

Now, if you wish to split the strength in half, you will use 25 mL of nutrients in the reservoir.

After, take the pH measurement of your new nutrient-rich water solution to ensure that it is optimal for your plants. Also, check the room temperature before you start feeding your plants.

9

GROW STAGE/VEGGING CYCLE

At this point, you have hung all the lights, calibrated, and checked the nutrients. The clones or seedlings are ready to transplant. All there is left to be done here is to get your marijuana plants to their permanent home for them to get started with the vegging stage.

You may be wondering, "what is the vegging stage of plant growth?"

The vegging stage is also referred to as the vegetative stage of plant growth. One thing you must note about the vegging cycle is that your plant life is actively growing, and its structure is being formed.

The fan leaves are growing bigger, the branches are getting stronger, and the root zones are expanding to future flowering sites. In short, the plant is creating the structure it needs for it to live, grow, and get the harvest you are looking for.

Here are three major things the vegetative cycle does;

Creation of root growth for total plant nutrition

If your marijuana plant lacks adequate roots, the chances are that they will not get the nutrition they need with the efficiency requires. Realize that plants require lots of roots for them to absorb the nutrient elements they need out of their grow medium – whether soil, coco coir, or hydroponics.

Foliage growth to absorb light.

Plants need an adequate amount of light to support the various vital processes of feeding and growth. They take in CO2 through the leaves for them to eat, grow, and breathe – and this is where the leaves are supposed to grow well for these functions to take place.

You can also get fertilizer boosters here to improve foliage growth;

Stems and branches

For the leaves and flowering sites to be present, they must have a place to grow, which is the role of the branches. When the branches are strong enough, they will lead to the growth of more leaves and flowering sites. Additionally, they will promote the growth of big buds on the plants as long as they need to be ahead of the harvest time.

HOW TO TRANSPLANT THOSE SEEDLINGS AND CLONES

Now, you know what the vegging stage is, and the next thing is to get started on transplanting your seedlings or clones into large buckets/permanent home.

The first thing is for you to check your plants and their cells to ensure that they are ready to transplant. If you are using perlite starter cells or soil in plastic cups, it is important to ensure that the medium is hardened and has lots of roots. This usually takes between 1-2 weeks. If using Rockwool, on the other hand, allow the seedlings or clones to produce as many roots as possible first. Ensure that they are completely soaked throughout the day because if it dries out, the roots will, too, is not a good thing. This, too, takes about 1-2 weeks.

Additionally, the light mustn't overpower the plants. For instance, if you are growing your marijuana plants with a light of 200 watts, you must ensure that you dimmed it so that the light does not overpower the plants.

Once you know that the plants are ready for transplanting, then get right to it.

Transplanting in to hydro

One of the greatest advantages of transplanting into hydro systems is that you don't have to worry about bigger buckets. Here, the DWC bucket in the reservoir they grow in will be enough to hold your plant roots throughout their life. In short, hydro systems allow you to simply transplant into the grow medium directly, and you are ready to grow!

Transplanting into pebbles

This is also referred to as the drip, DWC, or ebb and flow system. The first thing here is to ensure that you soak the pebbles at least for 8-24 hours before using it with an air stone. This ensures that they expand.

The next thing is to measure out the size of the basket needed for use. Fill it with pebbles until a quarter way. If you are using Rockwool, you can transplant young plants directly into the baskets with the pebbles. If using foam cells and the roots are below the cells, cut the cells off, and then transplant them directly into the grow medium. Ensure that the pebbles are filled ¼ way too.

What if you are working with starter cells?

Well, in that case, plant them directly into the pebbles as

usual. However, ensure that you keep an eye on the water for the perlite or peet to wash away. It is important that they completely wash off the plant, off the pebbles, and out of the reservoir as you change your feedings.

Transplanting rockwool into rockwool

When transplanting your marijuana seedlings or clones, you can go from Rockwool cubes to larger Rockwool cubes to get a complex network of strong roots. You can do it in flood trays. You must note that when doing Rockwool-to-Rockwool transplants, you must continue vigorous root growth just like when they were young.

In other words, start by carving out holes the size and shape of Rockwool you are using in the new Rockwool cube or trays. Then soak the cubes or trays in the preferred feeding strength at a water pH of between 5.5 and 6.0. Allow the nutrient solution to drain off completely. Then insert the cubes with your clones into the larger trays or cubes. Ensure that the roots are headed downwards.

Transplanting in a loose medium such as coco coir or soil

When going from Rockwool or cell into such mediums as soil or coco coir, it can be quite challenging. This is why you must exercise extra caution when handling the plant roots. You must never overfeed your plants.

Simply start by using at least a gallon or two pots. If you use pots that are too big, you risk overwatering your plants. The best thing is to fill the pots about an inch above the tip and then tap the medium to ensure that it settles down more. This ensures that any air pockets that form in the medium are taken out hence creating a "fill line" you must not go over when watering.

Once your grow medium is ready, make a hole in it – the size of your starter cells or Rockwool trays/cubes – for transplanting. Now, you are ready to plant your young marijuana plants in the medium. Then cover the cells completely with coco or soil. However, if using Rockwool cubes, ensure that you cover the cube completely to only expose the top of the cube. Finally, water your medium and expose your plants to light.

That said, realize that soil tends to take in water and to leave the Rockwool cubes to dry. You should frequently check your medium and Rockwool cubes to ensure that they are saturated as required.

To reiterate, if using nutrient-rich soil, it is not necessary to add more nutrients to your feeding schedule. This is especially the case because everything your plants need is already available to them – and then some!

There is no need for supplemental nutrients in soil-grown marijuana plants.

VEG: WEEK 1

This week is slightly different from all the others, depending on whether you are starting with marijuana seedlings or clones. This will determine the kind of nutrient mix you will use.

If you are growing on soil, you will likely water your plants twice a week. The first watering is with the nutrient mix, and the second watering is with plain water at a pH of 6.8. when growing your plants in soil, it is necessary to feed every watering. This **watering guide** will help you get it right;

If you are transplanting your plants to the hydro system, pay attention to the pH levels during the first week by following these **guidelines;**

There is a high likelihood that they will become acidic with time. Because your plants are still young, this fluctuation will not be drastic. However, you must cultivate the habit of checking the pH every day to ensure consistency.

Ensure that you pay attention to the PPM levels – between 200 and 250 for seedlings and 550-700 for clones – during the first week.

That said, test the pH every other day and top it with fresh water to maintain acceptable levels of your plants. Additionally, the lights should be no more than 24 inches above your tallest plants and no closer than 18 inches.

VEG: WEEK 2

During the second week, your plants are taller. This means that you must adjust the lighting to ensure that you maintain the 18-24 inches height of the plant canopy.

If your plants are in the soil, you must ensure that the nutrient strength you feed it with is at least ¼ strength in the feeding schedule. This is mainly because the forest soil is amended with nutrients already. The last thing you want here is to overfeed your plants and cause nutrient burns.

As the nutrients naturally get depleted in the soil, you can gradually increase the dosage over the coming weeks until you attain a full nutrient strength suitable for the optimal growth of your plants. Realize that some soil does not need supplemental nutrients – at least until the flowering stage. If working with soil, ensure that you use water with your soil.

However, if you are using a hydro system for your plants, this is the time to drain and refill your reservoirs for plant feeding. You must do this every week until harvest time – you better get used to it! Every week, you will drain the reservoir, refill it with RO water, add nutrients, check the PPM, and adjust the pH as required.

During this week, you must start pruning and training your plants.

Pruning and training your plants

This should be done around day ten of transplanting your seedlings or clones. While it is unnecessary to take many leaves off the plant this early, there are long-term benefits to pruning and training marijuana plants at this point.

These benefits include;

- It creates more foliage for your plants, enabling them to capture more light. More light is a good thing as far as plant growth is concerned.
- Pruning allows the plants to grow directly towards the buds during the flowering stage.
- Training allows plants to access more light, which stimulates the growth of flower sites
- Training maximizes the light coverage across the plant canopy for better, even, and controlled growth.
- Training controls the plant shape and height hence maximizing space in the growing area.

Topping & FIM'ing plants

You may be wondering, "what is the purpose of topping the plants, anyway?"

Well, topping plays a significant role in stimulating the growth of more shots from the main shoot at the top of the plant simply by cutting off the topmost plant shoot. This allows the growth of two new sets of leaves with new shoots, hence promoting more leaves and bud sites.

Topping goes a long way in training your plants to grow shorter than they normally do. This may or may not be a good thing depending on how you would like your plants to grow.

FIM'ing, on the other hand, plays an important role in helping the formation of more buds on the plants. To get even bigger buds,

When you get rid of 2/3's of the tallest growing plant shoots – at the leaves and not the stem – you simply create at least four times more bud sites when your plants begin flowering.

Be careful not to cut too much as this might only lead to 2x bud sites.

FIM'ing, in itself, helps your plants grow wider and shorter than they normally would.

Low-stress training

This is another important technique that yields similar results as topping as far as plants are exposed to more light than usual. This, in turn, promotes more foliage and formation of more bud sites.

Using a light string, gently tie the plant branches to the sides of the growing pots – especially when using fabric pots. If not, you can simply drill a hole in the plastic. If you can bend the main stem and tie, feel free to do so. Otherwise, you can bend the branches down – that works fine too. This way, your plants will focus more on growing stronger and vigorous instead of directing their energy to the main cola.

The good thing is that you can use thing technique to top for more vigorous growth. Remember, when you take parts of the plant away, it takes time for your plant to get back on track. It is your choice to consider one or the other to achieve your goals.

Sea of Green

Perhaps you have heard of big harvests using this technique – and that is true!

If you do it correctly, the sea of green will help your plants create large canopies for light, hence achieving bigger buds and many of them, for that matter. If you want SOG, it is advisable to have at least four plants. That said, your plants must note be crowded in the growing space at all.

Begin with low-stress training so that your plants can grow wide and not too tall – considering SOG is all about wide coverage. Then lay trellis netting above plants to allow them to keep spreading and limit the canopy height. As your plants continue to grow, ensure to "lollypop" prune them. This is simply pruning them for new growth on the main branches and other vital parts that support the growth of flowering sites. This must be done well, especially during the flowering stage.

VEG: WEEK 3

If you are planting your plants in soil, it is necessary to provide at least ½ strength of nutrients in the feeding schedule – especially when using Fox Farm Ocean Forest Soil or any other soil that is not super soil.

Bear in mind that as the nutrients in the soil get depleted naturally, you must increase the dosage over the coming weeks until you achieve full strength of nutrients that is optimal for your plants.

If you are planting them in hydroponic systems, this is the time to drain and refill your reservoirs. Simply drain the reservoirs, refill them with RO water, add in nutrients, check the PPM, and finally adjust the pH.

Nutrient lock and nutrient issues

During the third week of vegging, you must take time to go over all nutrient issues. Most specifically, check the nutrient lock. If your marijuana plants have been growing just fine and then you realize that they are beginning to wilt or brown at the tips, there is a high chance that they are suffering nutrient lockout.

Some of the causes of this are overwatering – especially in coco and soil. However, in hydroponic systems, it could be caused by mixing in too many nutrients – especially a dose that is too strong for your plants. The simplest way to correct this is to flush your plants and get the nutrient feeding schedule gradually on track this way.

But what if your plants are not wilting or browning and instead yellowing and losing their green color?

In this case, there is a high chance that the soil and nutrients used do not have all the elements your plants need. To correct this, simply give your plants the nutrients they are missing!

Pest control and fungal infections

If you notice that your plants are changing color to brown or yellow and that they have holes or burn marks on the leaves, there is a high chance of pest or fungal infections. Considering that the nutrients and surrounding conditions are stable for the plant, this issue can be difficult to spot. That is why you must keep a close eye on your plants at all times for even the slightest change in their morphological traits.

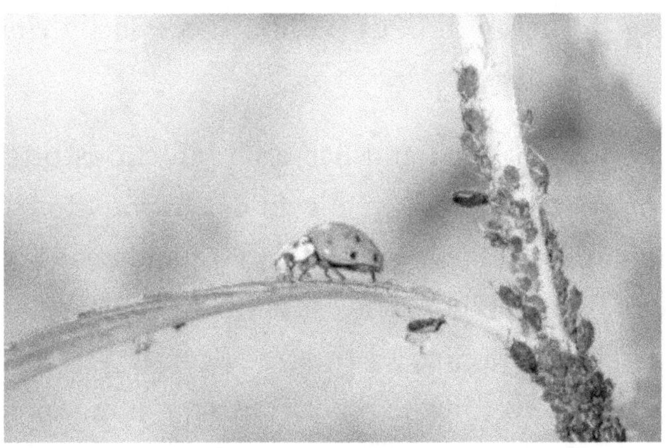

Pests are indeed visible on plants, be it holes or trails on the leaves. If you notice even a slight possibility that your plants are sick, the first thing you must do is inspect them. If you find pests on them, use natural pesticides to get rid of them. You could try natural soap and water as that kills bugs chomping at your plants.

Neem oil, on the other hand, will help kill spider mites. If you like, you can use natural predators – like mantises and ladybugs – to help kill bugs without necessarily rinsing off your plants.

Understand that fungal and bacterial infections often cause rotting of roots and eventually buds. If you find this out early enough, it is easy to spray them off and ensure that you keep them away using water, neem oil, or milk. You can also give your plant vitamins so that they can try to heal themselves fast. However, if the plant is too far along in an infection, get rid of it before it can infect other plants.

Synthetic versus Biological Pest Control

Management of pests is essential, no matter if you choose to go synthetic or biological. Synthetic insecticide resolutions will play a key role in keeping your plants protected from the damage that pests can create. However, they also pose a risk to other animals in your environment. And the pests will learn to develop a resistance to these synthetic measures, and they will come back with a vengeance.

On the other hand, if you want to keep your plants as organic as possible, there are also some potent biological solutions you can integrate to produce good results. These natural pesticides are non-toxic to wildlife, beneficial insects, pets, and humans, and they are less likely for the pest to build resistance. Another benefit is they break down quickly, so they have a low impact on your grow environment.

Basic Insect Control

The easiest way to ensure that bugs and pests will not infiltrate your cannabis plants is to use healthy, fertile soil. Also, controlling the environment through proper lighting levels, ventilation, and keeping your plants watered and appropriately drained will help keep the pests at bay. Be sure to keep a daily look on your plants, make sure they are clean from debris and pests, and keep them happy in a healthy environment. By doing it, you will get to the end of the season with the least amount of issues.

Aphid

Aphids are parasitic aphids (or aphids) that form a sub-family within the order of hemipteran insects. Like many other insects, it can represent a severe pest in the numerous plant species on which it feeds (nutrient plant), as well as being a vector insect of various viruses and diseases.

These are small insects of different colors (usually yellow, black, or green) with a size of 1 to 3 mm. Its body is ovoidal, and the three parts that make it up (head, thorax, and abdomen) cannot be distinguished. They may lack wings (wingless) or have two pairs of small, transparent membranous wings. In the final part of the abdomen, they have two small appendages that serve to secrete repellent substances for their natural predators.

They are usually found on the underside of leaves and stems, forming large colonies of dozens (or hundreds) of individuals. They develop a symbiotic relationship with other insects, such as ants or bees. Aphids secrete a substance sweetened by the anus, which protects the aphids from their predators. Something similar happens with bees, which incorporate these molasses to the honey they produce.

Aphids may need a single plant to complete their biological cycle, called monocyclic cycle, or may need two different plants, then the dioic cycle. They can also reproduce through eggs (sexual reproduction, females, and males intervene, which tend to be smaller) or asexual (parthenogenesis). Its propagation is curious because as the generations progress and depending on environmental factors are given different forms in the offspring, thus providing a vast degree of polymorphism. The metamorphosis experienced by the nymphs until the adult stage is minimal so that larvae and adults bear a considerable resemblance except, of course, in its size.

Whitefly

Whiteflies are homopterous insects of the Aleurodidae family (Aleyrodidae) that attack many types of cultivated plants, including cannabis plants. These are small mosquitoes with a 2mm long and whitish appearance, with a pair of wings that serve as a movement method. Their usual location is on the underside of the leaves (where they also lay the eggs, as we will see later), and, like other sucking insects such as aphids or woodlice, they feed by sucking the sap from the plants.

A whitefly body is divided into three zones: head thorax and abdomen. Like other insects, it has six legs and also a pair of white wings as a locomotion system. As we have said, it has a biting-sucking mouthpiece, thanks to which it can feed on the sap of leaves and young tissues.

This insect lays and fertilizes eggs, which it deposits on the underside of the leaves in an amount of 180-200 per laying. These eggs are almost microscopic, oval-pyramidal, and have a yellowish-white color. They normally have four generations a year (one generation is the duration of the life cycle of the insect, from the time they lay the eggs until the adult dies) depending on the climatic and hygienic conditions. However, in the greenhouse, they can reach ten generations a year, thus becoming a severe plague.

We can easily see that a greenhouse or a grow space will become its favorite habitat, as it is a plague that likes high temperatures and relatively humid atmospheres, being then the summer its ideal time.

From the egg-laying to the birth of the larva, approximately 24 hours pass; then, it will take another four weeks for the larva to become an adult, passing through 4 instars or larval-nymphalid stages, with scale form and located on the under-side of the leaves.

We can alternate our plants with others, creating an association of beneficial plants with each other; In this case, cultivating marigolds, Chinese carnations, or basil will help prevent the appearance of whitefly, as its smell repels them. We should check the back of the leaves regularly for adults or larvae, and use every few days a biological insecticide such as potassium soap or neem oil. Using yellow insect-trapping tapes, where adults will be stuck, will make things more difficult for these insects.

Caterpillars

During the outdoor marijuana growing season, many insects feed on our marijuana plants. In this case, we need to consider one of the most voracious predators that attack cannabis plants, leaving them destroyed and useless for their consumption, the caterpillars.

Caterpillars are the larvae of the Lepidoptera family's insects, better known after their metamorphosis as beautiful butterflies. Many species of butterflies are found around the world. There are many different types of caterpillars, with variable colors and sizes, but, yes, they all have precise characteristics in common, such as the segmented body, the six legs or the hooks of the pseudo path.

Before finding a caterpillar in our marijuana plants, we will see how the butterflies rest on the buds or leaves, generally in the highest parts where there are the most extensive and unreachable buds. The butterfly will deposit its eggs typically before the winter season arrives, these eggs will be born when the environmental temperatures are the most adequate, needing the heat of the end of summer which coincides with the arrival of winter two months away. It is feasible that the butterflies deposit their eggs, which are not born until there are suitable conditions for their development.

The caterpillars are long-bodied insects, divided into segments with varied colors, generally adapted to camouflage among the vegetation to avoid being devoured by birds or other natural predators of these insects. They move through its six main legs next to the 10 "false" legs distributed along its body, which can vary in position according to the type of caterpillar in question.

These voracious predators of green matter do not breathe through the mouth but do so through small holes distributed along the body, called spiracles. These holes lead to a network of internal tubes or tracheas that connect, providing oxygen directly to the cells, being a very active and spectacular respiratory system.

After doing the exhaustive search in our plants, we should do what we should do if we have detected a caterpillar or observe plants in bitten buds, to apply a product that repels or kills the eggs and larvae of butterflies.

Recommendations for a crop free of caterpillars:

- Divide the butterflies sitting on the plants.
- Look for the eggs in the leaves.
- During flowering, check the buds for signs of bites.
- In case of detection, apply a product compatible with the caterpillars.
- Stop applying the product within the last 15 days (before harvesting).
- Check the plants and buds after harvest and remove the infected or bitten parts.
- Collect the caterpillars that are born in the case of not being able to apply the product.

Thrips

Trips or Thysanoptera are a widespread problem faced by many marijuana growers. It is a tiny plague that sucks the sap from the plants of your crop. There are different species of thrips. They can be tiny winged insects (that measure millimeters) or have the appearance of small pale worms.

Regardless of the species, thrips are a nightmare for growers around the world. They can reproduce up to 12 times per year. Once they mature, they survive flying from plant to plant. Apart from cannabis, the favorite crop of thrips seems to be cotton, although they can attack many other types of plants. But they love marijuana. And when they appear in the early stages of cultivation, they are incredibly harmful.

The best way to get rid of thrips is to prevent an infestation from occurring. Make sure you disinfect the growing space entirely before you start cultivating, not only keeping the place clean but also eliminating any dead plant material.

Once you have started your crop, hang anti-insect adhesive strips. Like flypaper, they will trap most of the flying insects around them, which will stick to them. Finishing thrips once they have made an appearance is the only way to save a crop and prevent a new infestation. The best methods (without aggressive chemicals) are potassium soap and neem oil.

Fungi

If you happen to see any issues that arise with scabs, blotches, mold, or rusty leaves, you have a problem with fungi disease of your cannabis plants. One common way to combat these diseases is through the use of copper and sulfur.

Copper is the best option before you notice the infection or immediately after you notice the effects. You can get these in a liquid or powder form. You need to use the copper over the entire plant each day for seven to ten days until you see the effects wearing off of your plants.

The sulfur fungicide is as effective as the copper solution; however, it is not wise to apply this medium if you have high temperatures at your grow location as it may result in the burning of your plants.

Powdery Mildew

The Mildew is a cryptogamic fungus disease that results in fungal hyphae in plant tissues, wood, leather, paper, etc. Relatively similar to the Oidium, the Mildew delves into the tissues of leaves, stems, and fruits and not only remains on the surface as does the first. Being an endoparasite, we will not appreciate its structure until the damages produced in the plant are considerable, injuries that are visible in the aerial parts of the plants.

This fungus is part of the family of Peronosporaceae, which includes seven genera and about 600 species.

In agriculture, it usually damages potato, vine, tobacco, and Cucurbitaceae crops, without forgetting, of course, cannabis. It is quite a specific pathogen because each species attacks a particular - and relatively small - number of plants. One of the most well-known species is the Plasmopara viticola or Mildew of the vine, which was introduced in Europe in 1878 by the French when importing vine stocks resistant to the phylloxera, but host of this fungus.

As preventive treatments, we can choose sprays with;

Chamomile broth - 50 g of flowers per liter of water dissolved at a rate of 9 liters of water for each liter of preparation

Garlic - an infusion of 50g of garlic cloves per liter of water dissolved in a 1 liter of preparation

Bordelés broth, copper oxychloride, and dithiocarbamates are also frequently used as prevention.

Fusarium

Fusarium is the pathogen that causes Fusarium head blight (FHB) of wheat and other cereals.

Fusarium is the name given to a genus of filamentous fungi that live in the soil, in association with all plants, including marijuana. Most species are saprophytic, that is, they feed on waste from other organisms. Fusariosis is the name given to the disease caused by certain plant species of Fusarium fungi (phytopathogenic), which develop here as parasites.

They are a severe contamination agent in laboratories, and some Fusarium species attack cereals and produce myco-toxins capable of affecting humans, producing diseases such as Keratomycosis, Onychomycosis, or Panama disease, in addition to causing various types of skin infections.

Unfortunately, there is no valid or fungicidal treatment for infected Fusarium plants. Therefore, prevention is the best and the only option we have to avoid fusarium; we must be very conscientious with the hygiene in our culture, disinfecting clippers, irrigation tanks, sherds, etc. using them. We must start from a quality substrate, with known properties.

Step by step instructions to Prevent Cannabis Root Rot

You can reduce your odds of root spoil by taking a couple of precaution measures:

Have sound soil with the valuable organism and microorganisms' populaces. These populaces help keep the organism answerable for root spoil leveled out.

Water your plants effectively. This implies estimating the measure of water given to each plant and watching every day how they react to the measure of water given. It is smarter to see a plant start to shrink than to overwater during this procedure.

Have breathable soil. Growing in savvy pots and adding perlite to the dirt are two ways to help encourage the oxygen stream and enable the dirt to deplete appropriately.

The fine buildup is a typical sickness that appears on the leaves and buds of cannabis plants. At first, you will discover it on the lower parts of a plant where there is less sun introduction, wind stream, and more significant levels of mugginess. This kind of mold shows up as a white powder that sits on the outside of the leaves. When it shows up, it spreads quickly and can rapidly advance onto bud locales. Luckily, because the fine buildup is so unmistakable, it's uncommon for a plant to bite the dust from it. The fundamental concern is it renders the item unfit available to be purchased.

An effective method to Prevent Powdery Mildew on Cannabis

It's normal for cultivators to take a protection course with fine mold. Here are some best practices you should seriously think about:

- Splash your plants with natural items and fungicides
- Prune your plants to expand wind current
- Splash fertilizer tea or arrangements with differing PH levels to upset the spread of the infection
- Focus on which hereditary qualities are helpless to fine buildup and think about concentrating on different strains

If your nursery becomes contaminated with fine mold, there is an approach to expel it by showering the collected cannabis in an H2O2/H2O arrangement. By blending a modest quantity of 3% hydrogen peroxide (H2O2) with water, you make an answer that disinfects the collected plants and evacuates the buildup. This is a meticulous procedure, yet it can spare you from a tainted yield.

What Is Leaf Septoria?

Leaf septoria is a brutal looking malady that shows into first on the lower branches and makes leaves scab and yellow. It uncovered itself throughout the late spring when high temperatures joined with summer downpours or dampness from watering leave the foliage clammy. Nitrogen lacks can likewise fill in as an impetus to the sickness.

Even though leaf septoria won't slaughter your plants, it will decrease yields. When you see the disease, it's imperative to evacuate and discard the departs. Abstain from placing the tainted material in your manure heap to forestall future episodes. Showering plants with Bacillus subtilis fungicides can likewise help moderate the spread of the sickness.

Step by step instructions to Prevent Leaf Septoria on Cannabis

To counter the effect of this episode, there are a couple of moves you can make:

- You should have a perfect nursery space with sound soils. This is the most significant precaution measure you can take. If you have a flare-up, you may need to supplant your growing medium before planting once more.
- Tidy up your whole grow room, particularly if you're working an indoor nursery.
- Use trickle lines to water your plants, so the leaves don't get wet.
- Space the plants further separated to keep

coordinating dampness off the plants and the moistness levels down.

Root decay, fine mold, and leaf septoria are only a couple of the more typical ailments that can appear on cannabis plants. Different maladies incorporate the TMV (tobacco mosaic infection), fusarium, and verticillium wither. These illnesses have a typical topic when it comes to controlling: anticipation. Plant specialists must furnish plants with the correct supplements, microscopic organisms, and microorganisms to be prepared to deal with contaminations for similar reasons we as people eat well and exercise to forestall disease.

Hereditary qualities assume a significant job in directing how crippling an ailment can be to a plant. Watch your nursery, see patterns with specific hereditary qualities, and stick to solid matured hereditary qualities that are steady.

At this point, you must prune your plants further. It does not matter whether you are training them or not. What matters is that you prune to strengthen their branches to receive more light by getting rid of the lower hanging or even poor-performing growths. This will, in turn, redirect the light received through the leaves.

Bear in mind that leaves take in light. Therefore, if you get rid of too much foliage, you risk stunting the plants because they will not receive optimal light for their growth. That said, if your plants are damaged, they will try as much as they can to recover from injuries. However, if you prune them too much, you will shock them and hinder their growth. This is mainly because most of their energy will be diverted into recovery instead of strengthening the bud-producing branches.

VEG: WEEK 4/PRE-FLOWERING

How do you know that your plants are ready for flowering?

By the fourth week, your plants should be naturally ready for flowering. This is the time when they also start showing their sex.

For instance, if it is male cannabis, you can tell by their pollen sacs growing in between the nodes. If female cannabis, they grow white pestles in between the nodes.

It is necessary that at this stage, you ensure that you do a week-long flush of your plants – especially when beginning to show their sexes. This way, they are ready for flowering nutrients. If you wish not to flush your plants, you can give your soil plants more nutrients. If they are hydroponic, drain and refill the reservoirs with RO water. Then add in nutrients if you wish not to flush. Otherwise, you can use reverse osmosis machines to clean the water. Check the PPM and aim at keeping it between 0 and 50 PPM. Ensure that you also adjust the pH.

On the last day of the vegetative stage, allow your plants a

24-hour exposure to darkness and then a 12-hour light and 12-hour off cycle.

Think about it, when you do a 12/12 light cycle, it triggers flowering. Why is that? You may be wondering how that change in light exposure is possibly vital to plant growth? Well, it turns out that light is a big deal as far as vegging and flowering.

According to research, plants have been shown to possess a gene called Phytochrome Far Red (PFR), which tells plants to keep vegging. When you suddenly expose the plants to darkness, the gene changes to Phytochrome red, which is non-active. Therefore, darkness for at least 12 hours causes the PFR gene to be "switched off" to allow the plants to start flowering.

That said, you must bear in mind that when your plants are not exposed to light at all, that stands in the way of growth. While it is necessary to go all-dark before getting into the flowering stage, you must not overdo it. You cannot expose your plants to 36 hours of darkness because that is extreme.

So, what happens when a door opens, or a light leak comes through a hole in your grow tent? While this poses a problem during the vegging cycle, it is harmful to the flowering stage. If your plants are supposed to be in darkness but light leaks through, it will trigger activation of the PFR gene, which, over time, sends your plants back to vegging.

When this happens, simply take back your plants into the

vegging cycle and repeat putting them on 24-36 hours of darkness period for at least 2-3 days.

During the pre-flowering period, do the light cycles as follows;

Day 22-27, schedule lights on and off for 18/6 hours

Day 28, schedule 18/24 lights on/off cycles.

When the light is on, you must water and feed your plants as required. When the lights are off, allow your MH lights to cool down before you can switch the bulbs out to HPS. Turn off the timers to allow the plants to be in the dark for no less than 24 hours.

Remember that this is the last week of veg. The most important thing is that you pay attention to all the tips necessary in ensuring your plant's transition well from vegging to flowering. If you don't do it correctly, you risk delaying the flowering stage, resulting in delayed harvest periods.

That said, the best way your plants can grow is by taking clippings/cuts from the mother plant. While it is challenging to clone from a flowering plant, the clippings will take time to look as they should. Different genes are activated during the flowering stage as opposed to the vegging stage.

10

FLOWERING STAGE/BLOOM CYCLE

All the growth your plants have achieved since the very first day was leading up to the flowering stage. This is the stage when you will see flowers emerge. The buds will also swell before harvest time.

One thing you must note is that flowering properly is critical. If done the wrong way, the chances are to set you back to between 2-30 days. This is why you must pay very close attention to your marijuana plants and correct any issues that might arise along the way to ensure that they grow properly.

WHAT IS THE FLOWERING STAGE?

Note that the flowering stage often marks the end of vegging and growth of your plants' lives. It also marks the beginning of flowering that eventually produce buds you are looking for. Because of this, it is the most important stage of your plant's life.

The flowering stage is necessary for the propagation of your plants, considering this is when the pollens are released and received by the flowers to yield seeds. If the female plants are left alone, there is a chance that they will continue to grow their buds and flowers until harvest time.

From the first week through to the third week of flowering, your plants will continue stretching until they meet their peak height – otherwise referred to as the "*flower stretch.*"

The lighting here is supposed to be 12 hours on and 12 hours off. This ensures that your plants get adequate exposure to darkness for the PFR gene to remain active and keep your plants to veg even more. Bear in mind that the temperatures required for flowering should be 10 degrees less than the vegging temperature. The humidity is bound to reduce as well.

MIXING NUTRIENTS FOR PLANTS

As we have already mentioned before, this stage of flowering starts when you mix the nutrients required for flowering is integrated into the feeding schedule – if you have not done that already.

As soon as you start mixing nutrients into the soil, the concentration must be half the required strength. Ensure that you add nutrients to water every 2-3 feedings. If using hydroponic systems or coco mediums, be sure to use nutrients right from the start and keep using them as they have been used.

FLOWER: WEEK 1

Here, we are going to reset the days from day 29 to day 1. You may be wondering, "why is the flowering stage counted from the start?"

This is mainly because the vegging stage may take another 1-2 weeks for certain plants – including marijuana.

What lighting system are you using? Well, if you are using HID grow lights and have now switched to HPS bulbs, you are on the right track. If not, then this is the time to do so. You must ensure that your lighting schedule is switched to

12 hours on and 12 hours off to help your plant's circadian rhythm to start blooming.

What you will note differently on the environment chart in the flowering stage is that the growing space should be kept cooler and with a dryer humidity.

Plant maintenance

This is where you put up your Trellis Netting if your plants are growing too tall. As the plants start the stretching process – which will keep happening here – during the first month of flowering, your trellis net will go a long way in helping your plants maintain an even canopy. This ensures that the lighting distribution is even too.

If you realize that some plant branches are getting too tall, you must feed them through the trellis net. This will allow other branches to achieve a similar height.

The soil from this point going forward requires that you increase the watering frequency, considering your plants have become taller, and the roots are even larger. This means that the plants have a higher feeding capacity.

That said, ensure that you maintain the intervals of feeding and watering to prevent nutrient locks or salt build-ups. If you are not using super soils, then ensure that you use nutrients in all your feedings from now on. Ensure that ½ to full strength is used.

If using a hydroponic system, ensure that you drain and refill the reservoirs with RO water. Add in the nutrients, check the PPM, and adjust the pH.

Pruning and Trimming During the Flowering Stretch

At this point, it is necessary and recommended that the small branches and leaves are pruned off. This should be done at the lower one-third of the plants in your grow room. Here is why;

Increase breathability

Flowering plants like marijuana often produce more moisture in the grow room/tent environment. To prevent airborne diseases – like molds, pests, and powdery mildew – ensure that you cut down on the foliage and allow fain air to move freely through the garden.

Higher yields

Now, the remainder top two-thirds of the plants are supposed to receive more light considering this is where the majority of your harvest and high-quality buds and flowers will be produced. Realize that the lower third of your plant is too shaded from branches and leaves above. In other words, they take up energy from your plants to maintain the branches and leaves. If you were to get rid of them completely, then the plant will be forced to redistribute its energy equal to the parts getting most of its beneficial lighting.

FLOWER: WEEK 2

This is the week that marks the halfway point of your plant's growing cycle. At this point, the schedule should be your second nature. During this week, you will do the last pruning of your plants.

If growing in soil, your watering will get even more frequent as your plants become even taller and the roots larger. In other words, your plants have achieved an even higher feeding capacity. You must maintain the feeding and watering intervals of your plants to prevent salt build-up and nutrient locks from happening.

If growing in hydroponic systems, the usual is required. Simply drain the reservoir and refill it with RO water. Add in nutrients, check the PPM, and finally adjust the pH.

Maintain the pruning level you desire

Just to reiterate, this is the last week to make essential pruning maintenance of your plants before they can flower. Trimming and pruning your marijuana plants can be very stressful for your plants. Therefore, it is necessary and important that you do this task before your plants start using buds and flowers for 100% of their time.

Realize that any mass pruning at this point might greatly and negatively impact your final harvest and quantity of yields. If you have a few more branches and leaves, ensure that you cut them down at this point,

Here are two caveats to that;

The truth is, your plants will focus on the growth of flowers. Any new growth at the bottom of the plant should be trimmed. This allows all of its energy to go into the production of bud sites and flowers.

Look around your plants for any signs of yellowing leaves or even damaged/broken stems to get rid of them. If these damages are not removed early enough, your plants will focus their energy on repairing the damaged parts instead of focusing on flowering and budding.

That said, this is the stage when your plant's sex should be seen. If you cannot see your plants' sex, it might be time to go back to vegging. You must know what sex you are working with – whether male or female. If the sex does not show by the second week of flowering, you will have to reveg your plants. This is done by simply switching their light cycles back to 16/8 hours or 24/0 hours.

But what if you can already see the sex of the plants?

In that case, this is what you must do with your newly identified plants;

Are you looking to breed your plants? At this point, the leave plants as they are and the pollen sacs will burst during the second or third week of flowering. In that case, if you only want females, you must immediately get rid of all male plants. This is mainly because even the smallest bit of pollen is enough to stimulate seed growth in your plants.

If you are not sure what you wish to do, the safest trick is to separate males from females. Separating them from each other ensures that you collect the pollen sacs from all your male plants and put them in glass jars for freezing – for later use.

Then you can work with the females and maintain them all the way to harvest time.

Pest control

While we have talked about pest control before, you must understand pest prevention, regulation, and eradication. You must keep this list in mind even before you start growing your cannabis plants;

Cleanliness

Ensure that you sterilize your growing areas and equipment. You must wear protective clothing but also make sure that they were not exposed to anything outside the growing area.

Prevention

Ensure that you have neem oil in the growing area to use it as a way of preventing pest infestation from happening in the first place. Neem oil has been known to sterilize spider mites and other soft-bodied insects from reproducing.

When the buds start growing, you must be more meticulous with plant care. If you suspect that your plants are attractive to pests and that the flowers and scents going on are going to attract pests from all over, ensure that you spray neem oil to protect them from pest infestation.

Unlike pest control during the vegging stage, there are several caveats when it comes to pest control during the flowering stage. Here, it is preferable to use natural predators. This ensures that unwanted chemicals do not get into buds.

If you used chemicals before, try to keep off using them during this stage. The truth is that pesticides can leach into the buds and the growing medium in use. Once they are soaked and absorbed by the roots, they are hard to get flush from the plant.

FLOWER: WEEK 3

If you have not noticed, there is a chance that your plants will have stretched and grown significantly over the past three weeks compared to the first four weeks of vegging – and that is normal!

This is often referred to as the stretching period. Though it is temporary, the plants will finish stretching soon and start converting most of their energy into flowering and the swelling of buds, at least for the remainder of their growth.

There is nothing to worry about as long as you ensure the grow room is not leaking light in. Ensure that you keep a close eye on the PPM levels and the pH. As long as they are maintained at optimal levels, you are good.

If you are growing your marijuana plants in soil mediums, ensure that you maintain internals of watering and feeding to prevent salt build-up and nutrient lock. If using the hydro system, ensure that you drain and refill the reservoirs with RO water. Then add in nutrients required, check the PPM levels, and adjust the pH as required.

FLOWER: WEEK 4

At this point, you will see your flowers begin to plump up. The buds will also begin to ripen a little with the hairs coming up out of them. The aromas will become stronger and stronger by the day.

If you notice clusters of white salt rocks in the soil, there is a concentration of nutrients that have not been used up trying to mess around with your plants. At this point, you are roughly halfway through the flowering stage, which is a good time to flush.

You may be wondering, "what is flushing, and why should it be done this close to the harvest time?"

Well, flushing simply refers to the process of purging through the current growing medium to ensure that the plants get rid of salt build-up and excess nutrients they do not need. This way, the plants achieve a fresh balance of nutrients and water. The salt concentrations, pH, and PPM levels will fluctuate, causing adverse effects on the plants.

In using a hydroponic system, flushing your plants will help clean the plant pots or buckets, dissolve salts in the mediums, tubes, reservoirs, and pumps. To make this happen, drain the system of all nutrient-rich water and replace all that with RO water.

If you are planting in soil mediums, flushing ensures that there is no salt build up in the pots and within the soil. To ensure that this happens, give your plants RO water in place of nutrient-rich water.

It is advisable to do flushing at the beginning of every week so that there is no build-up for the rest of the grow cycle. This is only a 24-hour process, and once it is complete, you can get back to your regular feeding schedule.

FLOWER: WEEK 5/6

At this point, all you need is to maintain a clean surrounding and proper feeding. The truth is that these are full-blown weeks when your plants will fatten up more. It is necessary to maintain your pruning and reservoirs until the last week.

During the 5th week, you will notice that the bud sites will start swelling up and the 6th week, there is even further growth of buds. If you see new growth or certain growth dying off, ensure that you prune them off so that your plants are focused more on increasing the harvest.

FLOWER: WEEK 7

This is the week when you don't follow the nutrient feed schedule because all your plants need is freshwater until the time of harvesting. In other words, you are required to do the second and final flush for the remaining two weeks – almost 0 PPM.

The main reason for this is that as your plants start to ripen and reach maturity, they will produce lots of stored energy in the form of sugars within the leaves. You want your plants to cannibalize themselves to lower chemical nutrients in the final crops. This is something that will have an impact on the smell, taste, and overall quality of your plants.

The final flush plays two significant roles;

- Help the plants absorb the remaining nutrients stored in itself
- Flush out anything they would otherwise have taken up through their roots

Note: Any pesticides or toxins taken up by your plants will not be easy to flush out, making them hard to work with.

During this stage, the plant buds will ripen, and the leaves start changing in color. The leaves will turn yellow and begin to die off. The flowers and buds, on the other hand, will get fatter and start swelling.

You don't have to worry much about these events because they are normal. These changes are a sign of nitrogen deficiency, which is okay even though it is known to hinder bud production and growth.

FLOWER: WEEK 8

Bravo! You did it and finally made it to the last week of flowering.

At this point, most of your plants are through with flowering. This means that you must start looking into the harvesting of your plants soon. When we said all plants are different and that they require flowering times, we meant that you must check out your seeds and find out how long they take to flower. Harvest times often vary from 8 weeks to 12 weeks or even in other cases, longer than this.

If you realize that your plants are not ready for harvesting, ensure that you give them all the growing conditions they need to keep growing.

Here, you must keep flushing the remainder nutrients from your plants so that they are ready for their next growth and for you to enjoy the fruits of your labor.

That said, harvesting marijuana is tricky than most people think. It is not like harvesting fruits of veggies, which you may be used to. Therefore, here are some of the things you must know for you to harvest cannabis;

Harvest window

Just like most plants, cannabis has a harvest window. Think about cabbages for a minute – if they stay too long, they might bolt and become inedible. If fruits sit too long on the branches, they over ripen and go bad.

The same applies to marijuana. If they stay too long, they lose their taste and potency. Unlike fruits, sitting on the branches too long makes it hard to determine when to harvest or when not to.

The harvest window for your cannabis plants starts when the buds stop growing white hairs, and approximately 40% of them begin to darken and curl up. When you see this, then you know that you have about a month to chop your plants.

Here are two ways you can figure out when the harvest time has come;

Look at the pestles

When half of your plant's hair curl and darken, it marks the start of the harvest window, and that eventually covers between 60-90% of the plants. The only challenge is that some marijuana strains demonstrate different characteristics at different times. Hence, this technique might not be 100% accurate.

Observe the trichome under the microscope

If the trichome is still clear under a microscope, then know that it is not time to harvest. When they turn cloudy, it means that you can begin harvesting. When they turn amber, then start chopping them down. If you wait too long beyond this, the buds' quality begins to deteriorate or over-ripen, hence not making the quality of your marijuana any better.

What if your yield is not what you desired?

Well, let's face it. There are times when your yield is not ready when you thought it would, but that does not mean that it will not get there. You may want to wait a little longer. It could also indicate that the strain you are working with takes longer to flower. Most strains flower for only eight weeks, but others go to 10-12 weeks.

The best solution here is to find out how long the strain you planted takes to flower. If eight weeks is not enough, then feed your plants a bit longer for them to bloom. Once they do, flush whenever necessary.

There is also a chance that light is leaking around your garden. If you turn the lights off and you can see the light seeping in from the outside of the grow room, give your plants more growth time and darkness to compensate.

Finally, it could also be that they are under heat or light stress. If the environmental conditions are too hot for your plants, there is a chance that the lights are too close to your plants. This will stand in the way of harvesting with plants creating more growth, which is not desired at this point.

11

HARVESTING YOUR MARIJUANA

As we have already discussed, it takes at least 8 hours for indoor cannabis to complete the flowering stage. In the case of outdoor cannabis, it takes even longer for them to be ready for harvest. After waiting for a long time for your marijuana plants to reach maturity, harvesting time comes, and you are happy to eat the fruits of your labor!

Considering the size of your grow space, harvesting your marijuana can be time-consuming. This explains why most marijuana growers choose to turn to mechanical devices for harvesting, hence alleviating labor-associated issues during harvesting.

Just like other crops we are familiar with, marijuana harvesting happens in stages. Although gardens differ from each other and the harvesting techniques vary from one garden to the other, several steps every marijuana grower must follow when it comes to harvesting. How your marijuana is harvested and processed will greatly impact its quality, longevity, and potency.

If you ask any cannabis horticulturist, they will tell you that commercial operations benefit from streamlining harvest processes.

When efficient processes are in place, the cost of labor is greatly reduced while that of overall returns on investment is increased.

There are three major stages you must follow during the harvest time. These stages are;

- Fan leaf removal
- Trimming and removal of leaves close to the flowers
- Removing flowers from the stem

These three stages only address the physical removal of parts of your marijuana plant. The other crucial stages of harvesting include drying, sorting, and finally curing the cannabis flowers.

STEP 1 FAN LEAF REMOVAL

Once you see that your marijuana plants are ready, the first thing you need to do is get rid of the large fan leaves. These fan leaves are easily identifiable as the stereotypical marijuana leaves. You can pluck these leaves by hand, use a device like a hand-held hedge trimmer or scissors to cut them.

Realize that the large fan leaves you are cutting off do not contain high quantities if cannabinoids compared to the leaves that are much closer to the flowers or the flowers themselves. Because of that, most advanced growers choose to dispose of them. Once these fan leaves are removed, you have two choices;

- Trim the remaining leaf material while your marijuana plants are still wet – otherwise referred to as wet trimming.
- Start the drying process and get rid of the remaining leaf materials, either using your hands or an automated trimmer once the plants are dry.

STEP 2 DRYING

You must note that drying the cannabis plants can be achieved by either wet trimming or immediately the large fan leaves are removed – if you opt for the dry trim method.

You must take your marijuana plants and hang them upside down to dry.

You can also cut them into smaller, more manageable pieces or dry them as an entire plant. The ideal drying conditions for your cannabis are temperatures of between 65- and 75-degrees Fahrenheit. The required drying humidity levels must range between 45 and 55%.

It is advisable to do your drying in total darkness. This is mainly because the UV light from the sun or artificial lights risk damaging some of the high sorts after cannabinoids or terpenes in the flowers.

Generally, the drying process should take at least 7-10 days for your marijuana plant to dry completely. You will know when the drying process is complete because you can easily bend the stem of a dried plant as well as the stem snaps.

STEP 3 DESTEMMING

If you choose to wet trim your plants as a way of drying them, it is recommended that you destem the flowers and store them in appropriate holding bags for curing.

Alternatively, if you choose a dry trim and wish to use an automated trimmer, you must start the destemming process once the plants are completely dry. You can use a sharp pair of scissors to cut off the base of the flowers to remove them from the central stalk.

Even though most marijuana growers destem by hand or using scissors, there are several automated devices you can use to separate the flowers from the stem. Automation is something that not only makes the destemming process easy but also saves time if you have many plants – especially when you are running a commercial cannabis operation.

STEP 4 SORTING

This is one of the most important steps in maximizing the efficiency of your harvest process. When you separate the flowers into various sizes, you are in a better position to process your marijuana flowers more efficiently and effectively.

For instance, if you process the same-sized flower materials in an automatic trim machine, the trimming process is not only effective but also time saving and labor-intensive. When you automate the sorting process, this has a great impact on the harvest process, especially if you run a large-scale cannabis operation.

Once you have your cannabis flowers fully sorted, you can process them further in a trim machine, among other processing machines, based on size. You can also sort them once the trimming process is complete. Sorting your trimmed cannabis flowers based on size can make them more marketable.

STEP 5 TRIMMING

Once you are done dry trimming, a process that is often tedious and slow, and sorting, you can further trim your cannabis plants. The trimming process must be done using the right machinery to get that hand-trimmed look while still ensuring that you maintain its quality and save time.

During the drying process, you can stick the leaves against the flowers and hang them to dry, thanks to gravity's force. The main purpose of doing a dry trim, in this case, is to get rid of the leaf material that surrounds the flowers as much as you can. This will, in turn, expose the flowers, which are the most potent parts of your marijuana plant.

You will need multiple workers to complete the work in the shortest time when you do dry trimming by hand. The only problem with this is that hiring people is very expensive. In most instances, you will need to micromanage your workers and increase the security measures around your grow space.

This explains why most serious and advanced growers choose to use automated machines to do the trimming. Once the flowers are completely dried and destemmed, you can place them in an automated trim machine for a final manicure before they are taken for curing.

The trimming will have to take place during the drying process if you opt for a wet trim. Most growers often choose a wet trim because it is easy to access the leaves and hastens the process. For small grow operations – most especially beginners – it is advisable that the trimming is done by hand, and a wet trim is the most efficient way to go. However, in the case of large cannabis operations where most growers choose to use automated devices, trimming your materials once the marijuana flowers are completely dried is the most efficient way to go.

STEP 6 CURING

This is the grand finale of the harvesting process. It must be done once the trimming process is complete.

During the curing process, you must note that the flowers continue drying slowly. This is very important in ensuring that the flavors are enriched. The containers you use for the curing process must be stored in a cool and dark place where you can examine them every day.

For the first two weeks of curing, ensure that the storage containers are burped at least once or twice a day. This goes a long way in allowing some of the built-up humidity out and fresh air in. After these first two weeks, you can open the containers less frequently – at least once or twice a week.

After a couple of months, the curing process should be complete. Your marijuana flowers should be at the peak of their flavors. If you do the curing process properly, you stand to prolong the shelf life of your marijuana flowers – in terms of flavors, potency, and odors.

Just like the harvest process of other crops, that of marijuana has no one right way to do it. However, automation is quickly becoming commonplace among cannabis growers, and that requires them to follow a specific method to maximize both efficiency and effectiveness.

If you run a commercial cannabis operation, you must ensure that you invest in tools required for trimming, sorting, and destemming. These tools will help you remain in an ever-changing and highly competitive market. These tools will go a long way in reducing labor costs while ensuring that your marijuana flowers are processed fast and efficiently to preserve its flavors, smells, and potency.

12

OUTDOOR CULTIVATION OF CANNABIS

Cannabis has thrived in the outdoors for hundreds of years. As an aspiring grower, you should be able to try outdoor cultivation at least once. Perhaps, the main factors that can stop you from doing so include the law, the lack of outdoor space, and the thought of kids, pets, or someone else messing up your marijuana plants. If you are allowed and have the space to do so, then try it. Regarding kids, pets, or other persons who might mess up your home plantation, you can set up a fence to protect your plants from intrusion.

There are many benefits to outdoor marijuana cultivation. With this method, you do not need to buy pots unless you are going to do it on your veranda or roof deck. You can take advantage of sunlight, rainwater, and carbon dioxide as well. This also allows you to apply organic farming methods that are organic. All of these make outdoor cultivation less expensive than indoor cultivation. Cannabis plants are hardy thanks to their growth in the wild for years, so the preparation of your planting site should not be that hard. Another good thing about this is that you can yield more because you can use plants with better foliage. With such, the leaves can undergo photosynthesis that will provide the plant with more energy to produce the flowers later on. Remember that it is called a weed for a reason. It can grow nearly in the most random of places and sometimes, in the most random of times. The derivatives from outdoor marijuana plants are also known to have better taste and aroma.

To reap the benefits of outdoor marijuana cultivation, you have to spend much time on garden preparation. Getting all your gears ready makes the latter steps of cultivation easier and quicker.

Garden Preparation

It is best to start your garden preparation during early springtime. Make it a part of your annual spring cleaning. Instead of just de-cluttering your home, you should also get rid of the garden waste that the previous season left by in your yard once you are done with a general cleanup of your yard. It is time to choose a spot for your mini marijuana plantation.

Location

You should pick a location where your marijuana plants will

receive sunlight the most. Therefore, areas near or under the trees or the awnings of your home are not ideal. Additionally, the location should be away from areas where there is standing water. The plants will be under high stress if you do so. Aside from that, standing water may attract pests. You should also consider the spacing between your plants (3 to 5 feet away from each other). This allows your plants to grow freely and to allow you to move between them with so much ease. You should plan and set up the drainage for your garden when you are done picking the right location. If you are setting up your garden in a veranda or roof deck, make sure your plants will be elevated. The flooring may be too warm, especially if tiled that it may put the roots of your marijuana plants in high stress. You can elevate your plants by setting a platform using wood since the material is a good insulator of heat. You can simply create a rectangular box and drill holes where you will place the pots. Coat your wooden platform with a water-resistant finish. Make sure there are trays or saucers below the pots. These are meant to catch run-off water from the potted plants.

Soil

The first thing you need to do is to get rid of grasses or weeds on your planting location. The sight of these organisms might mean trouble, but their presence indicates that the site is good for marijuana plants. If you have other valued plants in it, transfer it somewhere else. Use a rake to remove debris in the area further. You do not want the possibility of a random piece of broken glass blocking or hurting the root of your upcoming marijuana plants. Getting your soil ready requires checking its pH level. You can buy a soil testing kit from most gardening stores to know the soil's pH level. There is no such thing as perfect soil for marijuana cultivation, but the ideal pH level of your soil should fall within 5.8 to 6.5.

If your soil's pH level is not within the said range, you have to improve it by adding compost and other organic fertilizers such as bone meal, blood meal, worm castings, aged manure, and bat guano. You may add some biodegradable mulch as well. Chemical fertilizers are more readily available, but they can hurt your soil in the long run, preventing you from planting regularly. Once your soil gets polluted, you have to let it rest for a while and treat it with organic soil amendments.

The soil type in your yard matters as well. The soil testing kit you are going to buy is likely to have a tool that can help you know whether your soil is clay, sand, or loam. You can simply rely on your observation, too. Clay tends to stick together while sand is too loose. Loamy soil is the most ideal because it may stick together, but it drains well, highly preferred by marijuana plants. Loam contains silt, sand, clay, and organic matter.

Find out what kind of soil you have, grab a fistful of soil, and squeeze it. If it tends to form a ball, it is probably clay, and you might need to boost the amount of silt, sand, and organic matter in your soil. If it tends to crumble, it is probably sand, and you might have to add clay, silt, and organic matter to balance it.

When you are done creating it, pour water in your soil. If it drains well yet remains moist, you have achieved the type of soil that is conducive to your marijuana cultivation.

Water Supply

Marijuana plants require lots of water to thrive. You will not have much problem if you live in a place where it rains a lot. If it rarely rains in your place even in springtime, you should buy an extensive hose or place a water faucet nearby. It pays to have a stream or other bodies of water near your place as well. You can get water from the bodies of water for free, but it takes a lot of time and effort.

Protection

Your outdoor marijuana plants have three main enemies: wind, animals, and humans. There is nothing much you can do to control the wind, but if there is a hilly side in your place, you may use such as a natural shield against the wind. If there are no hills, you have no other choice but to set up a fence. This does not only protect your plants against the wind but possibly against large animals and humans as well. That is not enough, though. You need to surround your mini marijuana plantation with thorny bushes to prevent small animals like rabbits from messing up your garden. You may also plant other taller plants, such as maize. Elderberry and bamboo are both good shields for marijuana plants as well.

Once everything is ready, you can start your hunt for the best strains for outdoor marijuana cultivation. While waiting for your seeds, decide the germination methods you have to employ. Pick at least two. For outdoor cultivation, you might want to germinate some of your seeds directly on the grounds. If you are opting for starter cubes, purchase them before you buy seeds. After germinating some seeds indoors, you can transfer them to pots for a while. Let them grow indoors first while the outdoor seeds remain. Keep their soil moist but not too wet or too soaking. For the indoor seedlings, give them 24 hours of light. Transfer them outdoors after 3 to 4 weeks.

Plant Care

After transplanting the seedlings, you are bound to face the most tiring part of marijuana cultivation. This requires you to be observant of how you handle your plants and how they respond to the care you provide.

Vegetative Phase

After the seedling phase, your plants will enter the so-called vegetative phase, usually in the second month after germination. In this phase, the plants will do nothing but grow more leaves and stems. They are going to need lots of water, nutrients, and sunlight.

You should water your plants every other day if it does not rain much in your place during this stage. If it rains a lot in one week, you might not need to water at all. When it comes to nutrients, you should provide nitrogen, phosphorus, and potassium (NPK). The ratio between the three macronutrients should be 10-5-7. Add some micronutrients such as zinc, molybdenum, magnesium, and iron as well. You can buy all of these from your preferred gardening stores.

As for the sunlight, you cannot do much about it. However, if there are trees in your yard that tends to over your marijuana plants, you should trim the branches of the said trees.

Pre-flowering Phase

The phase between the vegetative and flowering stages is also known as the stretch. This one only takes 10 to 14 days, though. (The vegetative and flowering phases take a month or more.) In this stage, you should gradually increase the water supply and nutrients you give to your marijuana plants. As to the nutrients, you should adjust the ratio of NPK to 5-10-7 or 5-50-17.

In this phase, you have to do the elimination of your male marijuana plants. Do not wait until the 14th day before you proceed with this task. Male marijuana plants tend to mature faster than their female counterparts do, so you should act as soon as possible. Remember to look at the appearance of the buds. Male buds tend to resemble small balls while female buds have hairs.

Flowering Phase

This stage may take 6 to 22 weeks. This is the stage where you can finally see the possible quality and quantity of your harvest. If you are using chemical fertilizers, you have to lessen the supply during the flowering stage to prevent the flowers from tasting and smelling like chemicals.

Stop supplying nutrients altogether in the last two weeks. In this phase, the plant will stop growing, but it will focus more on producing flowers.

13

STATES THAT RECENTLY LEGALIZED CANNABIS

U *tah*

Medicinal marijuana will be on the November 2018 voting form in Utah, after rivals of authorization dropped their claim in June. Even though the state has an enormous populace of Mormons, who restrict the utilization of liquor or medications, 75 percent of voters state they will cast a ballot for the activity.

Update: Utah voters passed Proposition 1 in the November 2018 political race, favoring restorative marijuana. However, the state will sanction an elective law. Partners on the two sides of the issue arrived at this trade-off in October to guarantee a type of medicinal marijuana arrangement, paying little respect to the vote.

The state's variant will change a portion of the subtleties

permitted in the voting form measure, including the evacuation of the home development arrangement and a decrease in dispensaries and qualifying ailments.

Nevada

Alongside California and two different states, Nevada cast a ballot to legitimize recreational cannabis in 2016, and the subsequent measures produced results the next year. Keeping pace with past markets, the underlying recreational permit application was open just to therapeutic marijuana dispensaries on favorable terms. Projections for open recreational market applications are when October 2018 and as late as July 2019. With dazzling early deals and an inspirational viewpoint, this might be another grower's most logical option.

Maine

Maine got one of the primary states on the east coast to sanction marijuana. Question 1 showed up on the 2016 voting form and passed just barely with 50.26% of the vote. The resistance requested a describe, however, rejected it because of cost and no significant differences in casting a ballot appropriation.

Preceding statewide authorization, a few urban communities in Maine (counting crowded Portland, South Portland, and Lewiston) have just sanctioned belonging and utilization of cannabis by grown-ups inside city limits.

The activity licenses clients 21 and over to have up to 2.5 ounces of marijuana and six develop plants. It's additionally the primary state to permit "social clubs" for cannabis to enable clients to expand retail recreational items on-premises.

Confinements apply. Guests to cannabis social clubs must utilize items there and not ship them off the property. In like manner, retail locations can't enable benefactors to open and devour their buys inside the store. Cannabis clients would likewise be not able to use off-site cannabis at social clubs. Offices can open when February 2018.

Vermont

Vermont is the most up to date expansion to the growing rundown of states that have authorized recreational cannabis. Starting on July 1, 2018, grown-ups beyond 21 years old have up to one ounce of cannabis, and grow two develop and four youthful plants in their home. The plants must be screened from general visibility, and just those more than 21 can approach. Inhabitants who are leasing need to get consent from their landowner to grow at home, in any case, proprietors are not required to concede authorization if they boycott growing tasks on their property, the occupant must go along.

Michigan

Michigan's association with cannabis has been combative since therapeutic marijuana laws were passed in 2008, yet the two activities to authorize cannabis this year each show guarantee. Because the state governing body continually reconsiders guidelines around medicinal marijuana, administrators are compelled to remain in business at the ever-present danger of arraignment.

While restorative marijuana is still accessible for occupants, an activity to sanction recreational utilize was not able to jump on the 2016 polling form.

Update: Proponents, as of late, gathered enough marks to get authorization of recreational cannabis on the November 2018 polling form. As per late surveys, 61 percent of voters will cast a ballot yes on this measure.

Update: In November 2018, Michigan turned into the tenth state in the U.S. to sanction recreational cannabis. Recommendation 1 earned 55.9 percent of the vote, authorizing the ownership and development of cannabis by grown-ups 21 years and over. The principal retail businesses will probably be open by 2020.

Missouri

Missouri is a longshot for those considering a passage to a lawful cannabis market. The state is without a therapeutic marijuana program or cannabis advocates in the state or official governing body, making sanctioning an impressive longshot for cheerful Missourians. While the state's endeavors to authorize CBD cannabis removes for individuals experiencing epilepsy and seizures, it is anything but a patient-accommodating condition. Just two non-benefit associations are allowed to create and convey cannabis oil in Missouri. This means a system of competent and experienced growers isn't probably going to develop very soon.

New Approach Missouri, the crusade to sanction medicinal marijuana, accumulated enough marks to get activity on the November 2018 polling form. It is anything but a slam dunk yet, however, as they are anticipating affirmation that it will be up for a vote this year.

Update: In November 2018, voters in Missouri passed Amendment 2, the state-protected revision sanctioning therapeutic cannabis. The new law permits patients who qualify and get doctor endorsement to grow up to six marijuana plants, purchase 4 ounces of dried marijuana, and have a 60-day supply of dried marijuana. Specialists can endorse medicinal marijuana for any condition they feel justifies this treatment. Income from deals duty will go to veterans' administrations.

On June 4, 2019, Missouri's Department of Health and Senior Services will make applications for patient cards and businesses accessible; it will start tolerating them beginning July 4, 2019.

Missouri authorities have not gone to an accord on whether therapeutic marijuana clients will be denied state occupations or welfare benefits.

Missouri voters didn't endorse the other two cannabis activities on the November 2018 voting form — Amendment 2 and Proposition C — which were likewise medicinal marijuana activities yet with marginally different insights about belonging sums and expense revenue distribution.

Oklahoma

Oklahoma voters passed State Question 788 in June 2018, legitimizing medicinal marijuana. The unavoidable trends are blowing through this red state, as they are one of only a handful, not many that enable specialists to prescribe cannabis for any ailment regarded fitting. Other states' therapeutic marijuana laws just permit its proposal for specific maladies.

A few changes to this law might be sanctioned, notwithstanding, as Governor Fallin stresses that this law has, generally, legitimized recreational use. The truth will surface, eventually, how this specific case turns out.

Canada

Our neighbor toward the north has authorized the clearance of certain types of recreational cannabis. Beginning on October 17, 2018, it will be legitimate for those beyond 18 years old to purchase crisp or dried cannabis, cannabis oil, and seeds or starts for development. Starting now, edibles are not lawful. However, that is gotten ready for some other time. The trading and bringing in of cannabis is unlawful, except for restorative and scientific use, which will require a license.

The law enables individuals to grow up to four plants on their property, yet plans are set up to permit bigger growing tasks, with limits. "Miniaturized scale" growers with crops no bigger than 200 square meters, or around 2,150 square feet, might be authorized. Breaking points on ownership, growing, singular areas can set age and lawful use territories.

Canada drafted rules for the bundling of cannabis even under the steady gaze of the law passed. Lawful cannabis items in Canada must have plain bundles with just well-being alerts, and one brand stamping permitted.

STATES CONSIDERING LEGAL CANNABIS

Arizona

Full sanctioning of cannabis endured a shot in Arizona. Suggestion 205 would have permitted individuals 21 and over to utilize marijuana recreationally. The measure additionally allowed clients to grow up to 6 plants. Even though the recommendation would apply 80% of duty income from deals to class regions and sanction schools inside Arizona, it fizzled. The voting form had 51.32% democratic no on the recommendation.

While it stays illicit for Arizona occupants to utilize recreational marijuana, earlier recommendations 200 and 203 are still as a result. The measures enable individuals with specific conditions to have marijuana for therapeutic use.

Connecticut

The table seems set for legitimization in Connecticut, with a fruitful medicinal marijuana program propelled in 2012 and an uplifting standpoint at a few surveys. Besides, law authorization in Connecticut is now getting ready for cannabis sanctioning and preparing officials to all the more likely identify and test for THC levels in drivers.

Rhode Island

Rhode Island bested Colorado, Washington, and each other state in the association for the most elevated level of cannabis clients saying they've expended cannabis inside the most recent month – for a long time running.

That doesn't mean authorization is a certain wagered for the small Northeastern state. Enactment pushed in 2015 neglected to flourish, and keeping in mind that surveying information looks encouraging, 2016 may not be the year the Ocean State completely sanctions.

States That Have Not Legalized Cannabis

Delaware

There's just a solitary therapeutic marijuana dispensary inactivity in Delaware, and only 700 patients enrolled under current necessity, leaving possibilities for recreational sanctioning desolate, best case scenario. While Governor Jack Markell did to be sure to sign a decriminalization bill late 2015, statewide authorization presently can't seem to occur.

Maryland

Maryland is attempting to actualize a successful therapeutic marijuana market. However, if state enactment presented a year ago finds a ground well of help among officials, a recreational market in Maryland may need to pause. Over 50 percent of occupants bolster statewide legitimization, yet almost certainly, the state will bolster a recreational market before its therapeutic marijuana business gets this show on the road.

New York

The State of New York is setting up a significant push toward executing a medicinal marijuana program. However, the weight applied to the only five authorized makers to grow and sell enough items by January could incite a deferral in accomplishing full legitimization statewide.

In June, New York moved to seal the records of low-level medication feelings to improve the conditions of those influenced by over 40 years of "hyper-criminalization." While this flag softens toward general demeanors toward cannabis, the way to recreational cannabis remains soundly through a fruitful sending of a medicinal marijuana program.

South Dakota

The "Coyote State" accumulated more than the necessary number of marks to jump on the voting form, however,

Secretary of State Shantel Krebs dismissed the petitions because not every one of the marks was legitimate.

South Dakota is the main state to make it illicit to test positive for cannabinoids regardless of whether the medication was expended in a state where it is legitimate. This "inside belonging" law conveys a stiff punishment of a year in prison and a $2,000 fine for sure.

ONE LAST WORD

Beginners almost always make mistakes. However, every step you take is a learning curve, and growing marijuana at home is no different. If you have been growing weed for at least a few years, you are better at it than individuals who are just starting.

In growing marijuana, know some of the mistakes that more experienced marijuana cultivators had committed when they first began. The following may help you avoid problems in the course of your hobby. Do not talk to anyone. Talking about growing your marijuana is a no-no. Keep your hobby to yourself.

Be prepared. When you grow marijuana, you may face uncertainties that can overwhelm you. You should consider the plants 'needs like nutrients, water, carbon dioxide, and light. You should also be prepared for other matters like lack of nutrient quality, bug infestations, and insufficient carbon dioxide amounts. Have a contingency plan in case your plants manifest negative signs.

Window growth is not enough. Sunlight is the perfect light source for any plant. However, growing your plants indoors and using the window as your only source of light doesn't cut it. Marijuana plants need as much light, and even sunlight is not enough. If you're growing them indoors, buy lights.

Even if your marijuana plants grow, they won't thrive the way you intend them to. Many fertilizers have an NPK ratio displayed conveniently on the packaging. NPK describes the combination of N (nitrogen), P (phosphorus), and K (potassium) as they related to each other.

For each period of growth, excluding the flowering period, you may want to utilize a fertilizer with a higher nitrogen concentration than anything else. When your plants are in the flowering stage, you should use a fertilizer with more phosphorus.

Growing cannabis in a nursery is comparable here and there to growing different yields, for example, ornamentals and vegetables. Cannabis, like most plants, requires the correct plant supplements, the right measure of water, and the fitting amount of light to stay sound. A controlled domain, such as a nursery, enables growers to meet these necessities by giving the capacity to control encouraging, light levels (daylight or artificial), mugginess, temperature, and so on.

Despite the similitudes in meeting essential plant needs to grow a quality harvest, there are a few key factors a grower ought to consider when hoping to grow cannabis, particularly when contrasted with customary vegetable yields. First off, cannabis must be grown to pass each state's trying qualifications to be endorsed for circulation and deal.

Perhaps the greatest difference I've found in the business between growing cannabis or different yields depends on the edge or gainfulness that the cannabis crop at present directions. From ecological controllers to lighting, light hardship, and coating choices, I see more cash being spent on framework than I have ever found in a practically identical vegetable activity.

Cooling is the ideal model. Customarily, most growers could never utilize cooling in a nursery. Numerous vegetable nurseries will utilize cooling somehow, yet it is ordinarily evaporative cooling. Why would that be? Other than nurseries being generally wasteful structures, most growers essentially can't justify the related expenses in a vegetable and elaborate activity. In the cannabis market, where item costs and edges are a lot higher, growers can justify a device like cooling.

No grower at any point stated, "I wish I had less command over this condition." Similar to the cooling idea, there are numerous instances of cannabis offices that are littler than ¼ of a section of land, yet they have natural control PCs that are north of six figures. Cannabis plants flourish in ideal conditions, and a controller assists take with excursion the mystery while limiting space for mistake. Cloud-observing frameworks, for instance, make it simple for growers to remotely screen dampness, temperature, CO_2, and supplement levels, and the sky is the limit. Each grower who uses some type of controlled condition agribusiness can profit by a natural controller, regardless of whether it's on a fundamental level of clocks and indoor regulators, or as convoluted and controlled as can be envisioned.

Cannabis plants are substantial feeders, much like tomatoes, and increment their admission when in the blooming state. Consequently, a supplement infusion framework that can nourish different zones is effective in eliminating work costs and guaranteeing exactness in the arrangement being sustained to the plants.

Typical practice with cannabis plants is to flush them toward the end of a growth cycle by bolstering the plant's pH-adjusted water of 5.8 to 6.2 for a few days, which flushes out all the compost from its life cycle. This guarantees the item is free of remaining salts, which is a prerequisite in most state testing rules.

If you grow any kind of plant in a nursery, you have most likely encountered a period in which you wished you had all the more light. A controlled-situation structure regularly has supplemental lighting to compensate for lower light levels throughout the winter months or on shady, cloudy days.

Numerous cannabis growers need to light for the full sun because there might be seasons of the year where they should have their light-hardship framework shut; however, they will at present need a 12-hour light cycle. This often occurs because of a light contamination statute. Numerous urban communities and regions have exacting zoning rules or guidelines concerning light contamination. Cannabis structures can be dependent upon extra prerequisites (smell control, road permeability, security, etc.) that can be incredibly expensive if not represented in the underlying undertaking stages.

Nuisance and infection control are zones often neglected, in cannabis offices as well as in vegetable activities, too. Nuisance and illness, the executives are considerably progressively basic with cannabis plants because of the stringent testing laws managing the market. A larger part of nursery vermin comes in through unscreened vents, but regardless I see numerous offices with no sort of creepy-crawly screening or aversion.

It's essential to have an arrangement set up to avert significant episodes as opposed to attempting to speed and battle a previously existing issue. This can be accomplished by presenting helpful bugs, or by executing a mist/showering framework at a convenient time.

Likewise, with all farming, there are no obvious responses for how to grow or how to make progress in the cannabis market. There are just answers of differing accuracy that will work better or more awful for every grower dependent on their circumstance and condition. The greatest takeaway is that growing cannabis, similar to every other plant, requires careful consideration and arranging. My best guidance is to inquire about your hardware accomplices, visit comparative activities, and gain from others in the business who can help bolster you.

Be active. Growing marijuana requires much of your time. You need to care for them as you would your child. Marijuana plants have short lifespans, from fertilization to harvest, and you just can't plant them and leave them alone. Make sure your plants get adequate ventilation, CO2, and light. Feed them, prune them, trim them, pamper them, and water them.

Not all soils are equal. A lot of newbie marijuana growers may think that any outdoor soil has enough nutrients for their plants. That soil, unfortunately, may only be 'glorified dirt. 'That soil may be too alkaline or too acidic and won't help to properly germinate your seeds. When you grow marijuana outdoors, infuse your soil with potting mix or fertilizer. Also, have a pH balance test to make sure the soil's pH is near 7.0.

Don't over-prune. Pruning a plant does encourage growth, and you may have heard that more pruning means more growth. It may be true, but you don't have to prune down a marijuana plant in its entirety. You may only weaken it or even kill it if you prune your plant too much.

Don't root-bound the plants. You may not know that marijuana roots grow fast. When the plants are placed in a container, the roots usually line the container's walls and go down to the bottom. If your container is too small, your plants can get root-bound, and they can die. Carefully transfer the plants to bigger containers after they have manifested accelerated growth.

Don't panic. The problems that occur when growing marijuana plants are from mistakes that can be avoided or reversed. If the plants begin to wilt and some leaves turn yellow, for example, it could be because of a missing nutrient. Some leaves will just die off either because of natural processes or lack of light. Generally, it does not indicate a greater problem.

Educate yourself. You will make fewer mistakes if you are well informed. Other people make the most mistakes before you start to grow it, so know their mistakes and learn from them.

If you don't have a daily maintenance plan for every problem, the truth is that you might get frustrated when one leads to the other. If unaddressed, you risk spiraling to another, and you end up wasting a whole grow. At least spend some time every day – 10 to 15 minutes – performing simple checks in your grow space to ensure that everything is working as required. This way, you will be able to keep everything flowing smoothly and end up with a high harvest grow and get ahead of all the issues you run into along the way.

So, what are you still waiting for?

It is time to get those pretty hands dirty, and after a couple of months, you will be smiling all the way to the bank!

Best Wishes!